Praise

'*Let Go Leadership* is packed with powerful insights, practical tools, anecdotes, self-assessments and step-by-step instructions that will equip you to identify the limiting leadership beliefs, behaviours and tendencies that can hold you back from creating a truly inclusive environment where every individual can thrive. It's not one-size-fits-all.

'This thought-provoking book puts accountability for talent development, retention and inclusion firmly in the hands of the leader. It will help you recognise your own biases, build high-performing teams and, ultimately, create an environment that is truly welcoming to all. It is a must-read for every experienced leader wanting to make an impact on DE&I.'
　　— **Pamela Hutchinson OBE**, Global Head of D&I, Bloomberg

'*Let Go Leadership* offers powerful and compelling insights and sets us on a path of self-exploration and reflection, gently nudging us to the fascinating SHARE Leadership framework and offering ways in which this can be sustained, all of which is geared to make leaders inclusive. By offering a wide range of insights gleaned as a leader and as a coach, Obi James makes an important distinction between diversity and inclusion, challenges many of our current approaches to leadership, and makes the reader feel comfortable in reflecting on their own leadership journeys. In doing so, she connects the reader intimately to their daily challenges, and while reading, one often gets the "that is me" feeling, making it so very personal. She also wraps the reader in an amazing sense of reassurance, by being non-judgemental, leading them to explore their own potential, and empowering them to unlock it. In today's world, this is a refreshing and radical relook at leadership, and hence a must-read for every leader who seeks to be inclusive and impactful.'

> — **Girish Menon**, CEO, STIR Education, recognised as one of the 25 most influential CEOs by the Charity Times 2019 and Top 10 Charity Champions in Global Diversity List 2020

'As an experienced leader, it isn't often that a leadership book makes me stop, think, re-read and reflect – but *Let Go Leadership* did just that. Obi has managed to write down what many leaders are feeling and thinking daily, and also give them a set of tools that are clear, practical and easy to implement. In a space where we often overcomplicate, it is so refreshing to find a simple but effective guide that can work for all styles of leadership and experience levels. I challenge any leader to read this and not find a paragraph that could have been written for them.'

> — **Melanie Seymour**, Advisory Board, Women in Banking & Finance

'Key to the success of *Let Go Leadership* is the access it provides to many years of real-life experience through Obi James's extensive work in this field. It shares powerful insights across a wide range of business models, with practical key lessons, tools and techniques, in an easy-to-read format. This, combined with a deep understanding of global shifts in the workplace, makes the book essential for today's thought leaders.'
— **Taponeswa Mavunga**, Director of Africa, Sony Music UK

'This is the book that I have long been waiting for. In *Let Go Leadership* Obi James guides you through an abundance of development tools and invites you to self-explore via the leadership archetypes. She also offers guidance on how to overcome limitations by sharpening self-awareness and applying her SHARE Leadership method. This book will lead you on a liberating journey to discover and trust your inner pioneer. Obi invites you to reflect and reset, helping your transition to fully inclusive and sustainable Let Go Leadership. Challenge yourself and the status quo – be a rebel with a cause.'
— **Melanie Grabe**, Director, Head of Corporate Access, Deutsche Bank

'*Let Go Leadership* is a leadership reflection and journaling guide. It is one book to read with a marker and writing materials at hand, because it so often calls for pause, reflection and candid conversations on our strengths and areas for growth as leaders. I found myself furiously highlighting leadership gems right from the introduction and thinking, "More leaders and leadership teams should read this!"

'While it is an effortless read, that should not be mistaken for a lack of depth. Obi successfully manages the delicate balance of writing a profound text while also making it easy to engage with the content. Obi's stories feel personal and relatable. They make this book read like a conversation with a trusted friend who's guiding you through the potential pitfalls of leadership. It gets you to rethink and reframe your approach by first acknowledging your own tendencies or histories that colour how you move through the world. Beyond leadership and the professional sphere, there are aspects of the content that are also applicable to personal relationships.

'This book will make many feel seen and heard, because it speaks to multiple leadership styles. In reading it, I felt seen, heard and challenged to regularly question how I show up as a leader.'
— **Mukhaye Muchimuti**, Chief of Staff to the CEO, One Acre Fund, Kenya

'I read *Let Go Leadership* just before starting my first managing director role, and I couldn't think of a more useful book to prepare me for building trust

with and empowering my leadership team. I'd recommend this to any new senior leader.'
— **Lisa Anderson**, Managing Director, Black Cultural Archives

'Through *Let Go Leadership*, Obi shares the insights and experiences that have resulted in her unique understanding of leaders and the dynamics of effective teams. As someone who has developed and worked with both small and large teams, the need to let go in a healthy and considered way resonated with me. The profiles around leadership archetypes helped me to understand my style of leadership and to recognise that I personally span several of the categories. With this awareness comes an opportunity to evolve and develop. This book will challenge you as a leader and, ultimately, as a person.'
— **Neil Rodford**, former Group CEO, YMU, and Executive Director, Voly Music

let go
leadership

how inclusive leaders
share power to drive
high performance

JAMES

R^ethink

First published in Great Britain in 2022
by Rethink Press (www.rethinkpress.com)

© Copyright Obi James

Cover image © Shutterstock | iam2mai

Icons sourced from the Noun Project:

Idea © BomSymbols

Quotes © Milky – Digital innovation

Writing book © Darri

To Dr Norbert Ezewuzie, my dad, my first love and my biggest champion. I miss you.

And to Adora and Abigail, my 'why', my best teachers and my everything.

Contents

Foreword

*L*et *Go Leadership* is a timely book, given the current need for leaders to be innovative in responding to unprecedented and existential societal challenges, such as the climate crisis, poverty, inequalities and a lack of social cohesion. In these uncertain times, inclusive leadership fuels real-time innovation and unleashes the full potential of all members of a team, while enabling continuous learning and collective responsibility for results.

Obi James presented cutting-edge principles that will take your leadership to a whole new level. 'Let Go Leadership' catalyses the collective leadership of your team, enabling each member to contribute their best self.

In this compelling book, Obi also inspires every leader to be authentic, by examining their leadership style and experience. She helps you reconnect with yourself, so that you can effectively harness and embrace the diversity of others. Through the leadership archetypes and case studies, you will identify why and how you should stop holding onto power, and therefore avoid stifling creativity and innovation. Obi also guides you through her SHARE Leadership method, which provides a practical blueprint for inclusive leadership that will start from within and deliver beyond your teams. The 'nuggets for reflection and action' ask you provocative questions that will unlock your own untapped potential, fire you up, and inspire you to lead in a way that harnesses diversity, builds collective engagement and ultimately creates sustained high performance.

Reading *Let Go Leadership* helped me understand key drivers of success in my global leadership roles, and in leading teams in Africa, Asia, Europe and the United States. As Treasurer of the World Bank, for example, I oversaw a complex financial organisation that managed multiple businesses that required diverse skills. I had staff of over sixty nationalities, based in France, India and the United States. We had vendors around the world, borrowed in 60 currencies and had clients in 130 countries. We could not have succeeded without applying the principles and techniques that Obi James teaches and so clearly articulates in her book.

We obtained extraordinary results in a fast-paced, challenging environment. We launched innovative instruments, including instruments to promote the sustainable development goals, the first pandemic bond and the first public blockchain bond. We entered new markets and transformed how we did business, because my leadership team and I shared leadership and empowered and nurtured our teams. We also had lots of fun.

I can also see that the successes of remarkable leaders who have shaped my leadership journey, such as Nelson Mandela, Madam CJ Walker and Mother Theresa, were no doubt catalysed by Let Go Leadership principles and techniques. These principles allowed them to lead transformational changes, innovate and leave legacies that continue to flourish long after their time.

Obi James is an ideal person to author this seminal book. It is the fact that she recognises the power that a leadership role comes with, and the impact each leader can have on their diverse people, that explains why Obi has built a successful career as a leadership and inclusion expert.

She also has a multicultural background and has worked with prestigious multinational organisations, such as Bank of America, Deloitte, Morgan Stanley and Northern Trust. The book showcases examples from her professional journey and presents examples of how you can obtain excellent team performance using easy-to-apply tools and techniques.

Let Go Leadership principles empower your people, who are your most valuable asset. Let Go Leadership fuels innovation and enables teams to learn and to respond to uncertainties in real time. As organisations fight to win the war on talent, leaders are called to rethink and reset their approach to leadership. This book is therefore a must read for any leader – whether in the private or public sector – who want to learn the tools and techniques that will enable them to gain extraordinary results and impact society in a fundamental manner.

I have no doubt that the Let Go Leadership espoused by Obi James will help society end today's leadership crisis.

Arunma Oteh
Chairperson, Royal African Society
Former Treasurer, World Bank

Introduction

This is a book for leaders who want to learn how to lead less. It is for those who have excelled as leaders and, as a result, now understand how much more there is for them to learn. It is for leaders who are keen to make change, in themselves, in others and in our increasingly challenging world. It is for leaders who are committed to creating a legacy of increased diversity and sustainable inclusivity at the heart of everything they do and are.

It is for leaders like Raj, a team leader and head of client services for an engineering company who I worked with in 2020. Raj was in a tough place when we met: the organisation was facing increased financial pressure from growing costs and cancelled contracts due to the pandemic. The employees were stressed and disengaged, fearful for their health, their families and their future. Raj was at breaking point. If his leadership team could not find a way to step up and reinvent the business, he feared they would all be out of jobs in no time.

I began to work with Raj, and together we journeyed through an incredible year of transformation and evolution, a process simultaneously undertaken by Raj, the organisation and the wider world. The pandemic forced us to confront the inextricably connected and interdependent nature of our world as we came to understand just how reliant we are on a multitude of invisible ties that draw us all together, whether that be rapid scientific advancement, enhanced technological connectivity or a greater awareness of our shared humanity. We learned the importance of being kind, to ourselves and to others, and we came to understand our individual responsibility as part of something far bigger as we fought to draw the pandemic under control across the world.

Through my coaching, Raj came to see how many of these global lessons now needed to be replicated in his leadership. He came to appreciate that same connectedness and interdependency, and learned how to use those connections to draw out the best from himself and those around him. By learning to share leadership, not only did Raj successfully lead the business through a remarkable pivot and transformation during the global crisis of the Covid-19 pandemic, he freed himself from his self-imposed shackle of leader's fatigue and, in his own words, finally got a life!

This book is for experienced business leaders. They have got to where they are because they have excelled at the leadership skills required of them. They have shown ambition, hunger and an unwavering commitment to succeed, regardless of the sacrifices made along the way. They have called the shots, challenged the status quo, broken the rules and, in the process, become powerful and admired innovators and problem solvers. They are probably much like you, and this book will teach you how to recognise, measure and celebrate these achievements. However, it will also argue for the benefits in sometimes stepping back and reflecting, letting go, looking afresh for opportunities for real and sustainable change for the better, and guide you through this process. Global events such as the Covid-19 pandemic highlighted how urgently we must change, but it also offered some heartening glimpses of the rich potential that co-responsibility for a better connected and shared world vision could offer us.

In previous in-house roles as a performance consultant and strategic programme manager, I spent time working directly with leaders on their people capability and systemic impact. I facilitated countless team building, talent management and succession planning meetings. This work clarified my growing sense that, as much as management and leadership training played some role in transforming leadership, coaching brought about deeper change. Leaders learned to recognise how their leadership holds their people back, and how this may contribute to the resource challenges, frustrating talent attrition, limited employee engagement and, ultimately, organisational performance challenges. Too often, coaching helped the leaders to recognise that they had made significant personal sacrifices along the way, including health, marriages and relationships with children and family. This impact fuelled my passion about the potential of coaching and confidence that I could deliver it well, and so was born my lifelong commitment to developing leaders, transforming workplace relationships and creating inclusive organisations through my consultancy and coaching business.

I have written this book to guide experienced leaders on how to reset their leadership and let go without losing out. You will learn everything you need to know to ensure that you make the decisions that are right for you, your people and your business. It will not be an easy process. To reset your leadership, you will have to ask difficult questions and undertake a self-reflective process that will feel hard at times. Exploring issues affecting inclusivity and diversity can be distressing; you may even feel attacked or guilty as you learn to acknowledge your privileges and responsibility and sit with your feelings. You will look with fresh eyes at what has got you where you are today: the long-established and hitherto successful ways of being and of leading, the thoughts and beliefs that may feel totally integral to your identity, and the hunger for power that served you so well but will hold you and others back unless you now learn to let go.

In this book, I will demonstrate that a truly inclusive world can only become a reality when we can all unreservedly embrace the diversity of those around us. It is not enough just to surround yourself with a diverse team: only through inclusive leadership will you be able to successfully harness the collective wisdom, creativity and talent that diversity offers. This book places inclusion firmly in the hands of the leader. It is designed to challenge your existing leadership practice while exposing the tendencies that can derail your efforts towards diversity and inclusion. It will take you on a developmental journey as you come to understand and implement a new and liberating way of leading your people and organisation as a fully inclusive leader.

This book is for you if you:

- Are an experienced leader whose business is growing and challenging you in different ways
- Feel held back by limited resources
- Feel like your diversity efforts are not creating the value you expect
- Need your teams to step up and take more responsibility for your collective success

- Worry about letting go and sharing power

- Struggle with employee engagement, absenteeism and talent retention

- Are drained by leadership, stressed and close to burnout

How to use this book

In this book, I share an abundance of insights, tools and techniques learned, developed and employed over fifteen years of coaching clients in sharing leadership and inspiring co-creation. You will also find details of my SHARE Leadership method and I explain how you can use it to become an inclusive leader who knows how and when to let go and build teams that are equipped with confidence, capability, independence and continual success.

To let go and become an inclusive leader requires focus and development at the level of self, team and your organisation as a whole. This book is split into these three parts. Each part builds on the last as you progressively move from learning self-leadership, to learning to share leadership, and finally, to sustaining inclusive leadership, even beyond your time at your organisation.

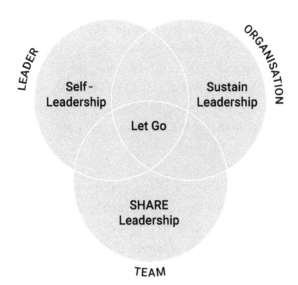

Self-leadership: The first part of this book takes you, the leader, on a journey of self-exploration. You will uncover and unlearn limiting leadership behaviours that stand in the way of sharing power, letting go and becoming inclusive. Strengthening your self-leadership will form a foundation for the journey ahead, and could become liberating for you as you come to understand that you do not have to be it all, or do it all, alone.

Share leadership: The second part introduces my SHARE Leadership method of developing and unleashing leadership in everyone. You will start to embrace regularly seeking feedback, introduce ongoing accountability to ensure that you are acting on the feedback and learn to adapt your leadership so that everyone has a sense of belonging. In this way, you'll reconnect with and engage the diversity of your people, empowering them to co-create with you from their own authentic selves. As you grow leaders and harvest leadership from your people, leadership becomes a shared responsibility.

Sustain leadership: The final section equips you to be a leader of leaders. You will start to look beyond your current leadership role to the legacy you are building. You will set aside feelings of anxiety and loss as you excitedly move forward with your people as you co-create an inclusive organisation.

Ultimately, this book will take you on a transformational journey, and I have introduced various stopping places to ensure this is a mindful transitional process. 'Nuggets for reflection and action' will prompt you to think about what you have learned and consider how it relates to your leadership. Each chapter ends with a summary section designed to help you think through the key lessons from the chapter and consider how to take these forwards.

My recommendation is that you first read the book cover to cover, and then use it as a reference guide that you can dip into when needed. I suggest that you dedicate a notebook to this leadership journey, in which you journal your responses to reflections, questions and activities and note key points to take away or that particularly struck home.

Note that in this book I have used stories from interviews, workshops and conversations with various individuals. I have changed their names and other identifying factors to protect their anonymity and for confidentiality, while not diluting the essence of their stories.

I wrote this book because all too often our inclusive team development programmes reveal that many leaders do not have the foundations and support that they need to move their expectations of leadership from themselves to their people. We also know that this century's expectations of leadership have changed. However, even with a global acknowledgement that diversity offers businesses a competitive advantage, many still shy away from moving beyond building diversity to harnessing the value it offers.

This is not a book about diversity. It will not teach you all you need to know about diversity. I draw on my own experiences as a black female leader, and what that has taught me, but it is not about critical race theory, and my choice not to capitalise 'black' reflects this. Instead, this book will inspire in you the confidence to make the shift towards inclusivity that you can – and should – be making. You will come to experience the liberation of knowing that you do not have to be an expert on all areas of diversity, and that through curiosity and inclusivity, you and your people can learn to harness the vast richness of your collective diversity. Inclusive leadership is a learning journey, not a destination, and what a fulfilling journey it can be!

PART ONE
SELF-LEADERSHIP

When I decided to move the focus of my leadership development consultancy from developing individual leaders to creating inclusive teams, I had not anticipated the resistance that would come from leaders faced with sharing power and letting go.

Initially, my intention was to build organisational inclusivity by just creating networks of inclusive leadership teams within organisations. By the end of delivering the first handful of our Inclusive Leadership Team development programmes, working with team members collectively, my team of associates and I realised that more was needed to get these teams ready to become inclusive. The resistance from the leaders of teams was like nothing I had come across in my fifteen years of people and leadership development. It felt like we were being faced with leaders all suffering from 'imposter syndrome on steroids'.

As I took a step back to hear and understand what lay behind these experienced leaders' resistance, my empathy for leaders and the daily internal challenges they face intensified. This led to the decision to expand our offering by re-introducing our Inclusive Leader programmes designed to coach leaders on a one-to-one basis and move them from feeling threatened by their high-potential team members, to nurturing and empowering these talented future leaders so that, together, they could take their organisations to new heights. I realised that, as much as the leaders and their teams might desire to share the power that leadership affords them, most were not ready. We needed to put a lot of work into preparing the leaders to step aside, step back, or in some cases, let go altogether. Self-leadership was a crucial prerequisite for leaders to share leadership, sustain leadership and build inclusion.

As I worked with the leadership teams collectively, my colleagues coached individual leaders to develop their confidence in letting go and embracing shared leadership to stop limiting their organisation's progression. Our one-to-one work with these leaders not only proved that the leaders themselves needed unique support, but also led to the birth of this book. It is intended to accompany our Inclusive Team

Development programmes, as pre-reading for every leader who wants to be inclusive but is not equipped to make that vision a reality.

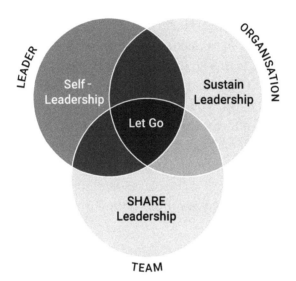

Inclusive leaders see difference as an opportunity, rather than a threat. They know they need diversity to meet the future head-on and drive sustainable high performance. Inclusive leaders share leadership and power. For them, it's not just a catchphrase or a mission statement; it's how they work, every day. If someone has a different idea from yours or challenges the status quo, you listen and learn from them. If your people always agree with you, you pause to check in on how inclusive you are being or on how much diversity you have.

If you have a disability, are from a racialised group, feel disadvantaged by your age, gender or sexuality, or are from a nondominant group, it is important to know that you can feel a sense of belonging in any workplace that prioritises inclusion. And if you are a leader, you have what is needed to lay the right foundation and build teams that attract, welcome and nurture diversity. If you read this book and fully embrace Let Go Leadership, you will move from the traditional command-and-control leadership approach to one of shared leadership that will not only empower your people, but will free you up to seek and embrace a more strategic and inclusive leadership that will excite you while taking your organisation to the next level.

1
The Leadership Archetypes

Archetypes are the frequently occurring patterns that we most readily recognise in others. Having assessed, studied and developed leaders for over fifteen years, I have come across a variety of leadership tendencies and styles, and learned about their respective impact on inclusion in teams and organisations.

We all have strengths that we bring to the table. We also all have blind spots that can undermine our success as inclusive leaders and thus our ability to lead our teams and organisations effectively. I have successfully narrowed all the leadership tendencies that I have come across into nine archetypes, each describing a range of behaviours that influence a particular leadership style. There is no good or bad archetype, and I have described each in a way that highlights both its pros and cons. I have identified the following nine archetypes:

1. The commander	6. The joker
2. The innovator	7. The pleaser
3. The protector	8. The perfectionist
4. The hero	9. The problem solver
5. The wanderer	

In this chapter, you will be introduced to my leadership archetypes, which I have developed based on my work with over 1,000 leaders across various organisations and sectors. You will reflect on your leadership, then identify your archetype, how it serves you and how it gets in the way. Most importantly, you will look at ways to adapt your leadership so that as you let go, your people step up and, collectively, you can successfully move forward.

When you reflect on whichever archetype (or combination of archetypes) you most identify with, you will trace its development in your own experiences of leadership, even all the way back to how you were raised by your parents and/or carers in childhood. With this self-awareness, as well as an understanding of the other archetypes in your team and organisation, you will become more intentional about maximising your diverse strengths.

You will also find that an organisation may inadvertently attract more of certain types of archetypes than others, based on its culture, marketing and recruitment processes. All these factors can influence recurring patterns of behaviour that affect how effective you are as an inclusive leader, team or organisation.

Read through all the archetypes and pay attention to which one(s) you feel most represents you as a leader:

1. The commander

The commander craves power and control. They are used to calling the shots and trying to oversee and drive everything. They are really challenged by anyone that steps up, and pride themselves on being decisive and getting things done. They seem to know it all and leave little or no room for mistakes.

As a leader, the commander has probably had to work hard to prove themselves, get to their current level of leadership and create success. They often find it hard to let go.

Good at: Showing strength and getting things done

Drive: Power, structure and results

Strategy: Command, order and whatever it takes

What they tell themselves: 'If I don't take care of anything, it doesn't get done properly'

Fear: Failure or dependency on others

Leadership struggle: Anxiety which can rub off on those around them, being vulnerable, connecting with others, empowering others

Unintended impact as a leader: Fear, stress and demotivation

2. The innovator

The innovator loves creativity and newness. They thrive on the excitement of coming up with new and pioneering ideas, products and services. They are often able to see conflict as positive, as it births new possibilities. The innovator has probably experienced freedom in their own work and gained a reputation as a genius. They get bored easily and are always on the lookout for new ideas.

Good at: Creativity, generating ideas and solutions to complex problems

Drive: Disruption and innovation

Strategy: Unpick everything, create and recreate

What they tell themselves: 'I can come up with even newer solutions'

Fear: Mediocrity

Leadership struggle: Being mindful, letting go of the need to make improvements, celebrating the journey not the destination

Unintended impact as a leader: Overwhelm, disengagement due to constant changes, a lack of commitment or trust in sustainability of solutions

3. The protector

The protector is driven by the need to keep everyone safe. They like to ensure everyone stays out of trouble and will come forward at the slightest hiccup in any relationship. They feel power in fighting for and taking care of their people.

The protector has probably had to take care of others and keep the peace in the past. They overextend themselves in service of others and inadvertently build a dependency on themselves.

Good at: Checking in on and rescuing people

Drive: Love, connection and security

Strategy: Take care of everyone

What they tell themselves: 'I should look out for everyone'

Fear: Anyone getting hurt or letting people down

Leadership struggle: Allowing people to stand up for themselves, constructively challenging their people and managing poor performance

Unintended impact as a leader: Can hold people back by not providing constructive feedback, coaching them to take risks, aim high and break boundaries

4. The hero

The hero constantly wants to prove themselves. They enjoy saving the day and often get an ego boost from clearing up other people's mess. The hero is motivated to tackle chaos and can inadvertently stir up anxiety or conflict so they can make things better again. They strive to be relevant and admired.

Good at: Restoring order

Drive: To be extraordinary

Strategy: Get there on time to save the day

What they tell themselves: 'Things are often a mess until I come along!'

Fear: Weakness, needing others and not being needed

Leadership struggle: Stepping back and coaching, listening, can be too eager to bring solutions, personal exhaustion and work-life balance

Unintended impact as a leader: Disempowering, stifles resilience, builds dependency

5. The wanderer

The wanderer is willing to try anything once, but often does not follow through. They suffer from what

is known as 'shiny object syndrome' – the moment they learn about something new, they rush off to implement it. They throw everything at it... that is, until something even newer comes along.

The wanderer often comes from a place of wanting to belong themselves. They always want more and often suffer from FOMO (fear of missing out).

Good at: Spotting new trends and keeping an eye on tomorrow while tackling today

Drive: To find the 'next best thing'

Strategy: Always looking out for new opportunities

What they tell themselves: 'Nothing is quite ready'

Fear: Conformity, missing out

Leadership struggle: Commitment and completion

Unintended impact as a leader: Initially captivating, but can become frustrating over time, leading to demotivated or disengaged employees

6. The joker

The joker loves light-hearted fun, humour and silliness. They often love people and like to be seen as entertaining.

The joker often has history of wanting to be liked and accepted. They draw attention to themselves through their jokes and exuberance.

Good at: Bringing in lightness and making the work environment fun

Drive: Enjoyment and making people laugh

Strategy: Bring in playfulness

What they tell themselves: 'I have to be fun'

Fear: Being seen as boring or being bored

Leadership struggle: Being taken seriously, building trust and confidence in decisions

Unintended impact as a leader: Can be seen as frivolous and lacking authority

7. The pleaser

The pleaser wants to be everyone's best friend. They hate the thought of anyone not liking them and go out of their way to prove that they are there for everyone. Unlike the protector, they do not necessarily feel that they can provide safety or security. They bring a particularly nurturing approach to their interactions.

Good at: Building engagement and fulfilment in their people

Drive: To make everyone happy

Strategy: Service to others

What they tell themselves: 'It's my job to ensure people are happy'

Fear: Letting people down

Leadership struggle: Setting clear boundaries, holding others accountable and self-care

Unintended impact as a leader: Can struggle with providing constructive feedback, can give poor performers a false sense of confidence in their abilities and stifle their development and progression

8. The perfectionist

Perfectionists are committed to excellence. They like to ensure all i's are dotted and t's crossed. Ironically, their aversion to risk and avoidance of mistakes means that they hold themselves and their people back.

The perfectionist has probably experienced a fear-inducing commander style of leadership or culture themselves. Although different, they can fuel similar insecurities in their people as the commander does in theirs.

Good at: Analysis, due diligence and risk assessment

Drive: Perfection

Strategy: Always checking and cross-checking

What they tell themselves: 'It's not yet perfect or even good enough'

Fear: If they relax their guard, they are likely to get in trouble

Leadership struggle: Often gets stuck and struggles to sign off on projects to get them to completion

Unintended impact as a leader: Demotivating, as there's always something not quite right, can make their people question themselves

9. The problem solver

The problem solver is happiest when they identify the solution to a problem. They are often deep in thought, trying to access whatever knowledge they have to offer and share.

The problem solver can become a worrier who dwells too much, and sometimes unnecessarily, on problems in their quest for solutions. They struggle with delegating and find it difficult to say, 'I don't know.'

Good at: Analysis and finding solutions

Drive: Finding the answers

Strategy: Seeking information and knowledge

What they tell themselves: 'I need to figure this out'

Fear: Being perceived as ignorant

Leadership struggle: Being present, patience, connecting with others

Unintended impact as a leader: Can be pedantic, disempowering, can stifle creativity

Found your archetype?

Having gone through the archetypes, you will most likely find that one resonates particularly strongly with you. You may find that you can relate to a combination of them, but usually there will be one archetype dominating and influencing how you show up as a leader.

Within your team members, you may find that there is a predominant archetype. Without attention, a group of individuals with similar qualities and tendencies might exert a disproportionate amount of influence on your opinions, decisions and culture. This can get in the way of you being inclusive. For example, if you are in a group of predominantly protectors and/or pleasers, you'll probably come out thinking the lack of conflict in your team is great. However, the innovator who appreciates a good challenge might feel excluded.

Working with your team members to identify the archetypes within your team means you can use these archetypes and what we know of them when designing how leadership is best shared and harnessed within your team.

As a leader, a good place to look for some clues about your archetype would be any 360-feedback report you may have. With the archetypes in mind, re-read your report and identify which archetype relates closely to your leadership impact.

 NUGGETS FOR REFLECTION AND ACTION

Reflect on and journal your responses to the following:

- Which archetypes, qualities or preferences do you identify most with?
- Which archetypes are dominant or missing in your team?
- Building on the archetype, can you identify your own tendencies or blind spots that could get in the way of your inclusive leadership?
- Who will hold you accountable to ensure that these do not limit inclusion?

 **Key lessons**

In this chapter, you have explored the nine leadership archetypes. You have learned that:

- Identifying your leadership archetype will help discover your strengths, leadership gaps and blind spots.

- If your team is made up of members that predominantly fall under the same archetypes, this could fuel groupthink (discussed later).

- Without a diversity of archetypes, your team might inadvertently attract and hire people that are more like you, and marginalise and exclude those less like you.

Having looked at the leadership archetypes and identified some of your own tendencies, you will already be recognising how they might be getting in the way of your sharing leadership and being inclusive. Over the next three chapters, I will introduce some other reasons why leaders do not share, discuss why it is important for leaders to share, and most importantly, cover how to get ready to share and to become a truly inclusive leader.

2
Why Leaders Do
Not Share

'I have worked my way up within this organisation and have earned my place as the go-to person whenever anyone feels stuck,' said Sam.

'Interesting,' I reply.

This was our second executive coaching session, and I could already see the disconnect between Sam and their team members. Sam's internal 360-degree feedback report showed a relatively low score on the leadership behaviours associated with team members feeling that their 'ideas were respected'. Through coaching, Sam was able to start challenging their own instinctive behaviours, letting go of perfectionism, and fighting their usual tendencies towards rescuing everyone and needing to be the hero.

The adage 'With great power comes great responsibility' has been used for centuries – and with good reason. Contrary to what you may think, your leadership role does not afford you a monopoly or exclusive rights to leadership. It is a privilege which comes with great responsibility. Part of that is to share. Leaders often resist sharing leadership because it means stepping out of their comfort zone. Many may feel that they have had to work exceptionally hard to prove that they are good at what they do. Letting go of, or sharing, these hard-earned responsibilities creates space for what they have yet to learn, and with that exposure comes insecurities.

In this chapter, you will learn more about the behaviours that held Sam back. You will come to understand more about the mindset and resulting behaviours that get in the way of leaders sharing power. Most importantly, you will learn to identify what holds you back, and as you work through the chapters to come, you will gather tools and techniques to tackle some of those self-limiting behaviours.

The saboteur voice

During my coaching development training with The Co-Active Training Institute, I was introduced to the concept of the 'saboteur' as a brilliant way to think about that self-sabotaging inner voice or voices that hold us back. I have since learned that the word comes from *sabot*, French for a wooden shoe, and that the term 'saboteur' comes from an old story about disgruntled workers who threw their wooden shoes into the work machinery during a strike. They quit.

Saboteurs are those voices in our head that get in the way of our progression. They stifle our ideas and make us quit before we have tried enough, or even at all. A large part of your saboteur's job is to keep you within your comfort zones. It runs a commentary in your head, getting louder and louder the closer you get to making a change. It keeps you hooked to old ways of doing things and convinces you that change is anything from too complicated to impossible. You have probably already heard your saboteur's voice while reading this book.

First, most people (if not all) have saboteurs. Mine got loud as I typed up my resignation letter when I left my corporate job to set up my coaching and consultancy business. I can still hear her, bellowing in my ear: 'Why would you leave a successful, well-paid VP role, with all the security it affords you, to jump into self-employment?' My saboteur voice emphasised the potentially disastrous consequences so heavily that I was practically picturing myself lying desolate on the streets of London, begging for money to feed my family.

Sound familiar? Those thoughts telling you that you are not good enough, clever enough, ready enough, etc? Here's the good news – it's normal. Saboteurs feed the universal self-doubt that we all have. The difference between a confident and successful person often lies in their ability to tackle their saboteur. You can put them right back in their box.

In this chapter, you will learn more about your saboteurs and the tendencies that get in the way of leaders sharing leadership. As you go through the next few chapters, you will identify your own tendencies and develop strategies to prevent them from holding you back. For now, let's look at the impact of one of the most common saboteur-driven tendencies that gets in the way of leaders being inclusive: perfectionism.

Perfectionism

If, like me, you have perfectionist tendencies, you are probably too hard on yourself. You strive to have everything the best it can be, and yet, as a leader, you struggle to find the time to be perfect at *everything*. You firmly believe that you are the only one capable of getting certain things done to the standards that you expect and require. You take pride in your ability to challenge and push your people, encouraging them to be the best that they can possibly be. However, you might miss that you are taking it all too far.

Perfection is a myth. It is a state that cannot be obtained, but in your quest to reach it, you continually move the goalpost, frustrating yourself in the process. Perfection is a goalpost that will constantly be moved until our last days. Embracing this can be positive, but it is hard to do unless you have learned to be kind to yourself. This means acknowledging and accepting mistakes as a crucial part of your learning journey and learning to let go of unhealthy expectations – not just of yourself, but of others. Otherwise, you may inadvertently extend those unhealthy expectations to your people and end up with team(s) that are too hard on themselves and feel demotivated. To stay on course as an inclusive leader, you will have to embrace this lifelong learning experience, using knowledge gained from failed experiences to fuel progression.

The aspiration and drive to perfection can only be positive when it provides a stretch, but does not slow down progression, collaboration and the overall wellbeing and balance of your team members. A good leader stretches their people, but not at the risk of breaking them. Too often, a leader's need for perfection and fear of risk-taking can stand in the way of empowering people to find their own creative problem-solving solutions, hence marginalising diversity.

Time

Inclusive leadership requires that you dedicate ample time to developing leadership, not just in yourself but in others. On countless occasions I have heard new leadership coaching clients comment, 'It will take me twice as long to train someone to do something, so it is easier for me to do it myself.' Although perhaps true, this is creating a false sense of economy which, if left unchallenged, leaves leaders holding on to unnecessary aspects of their roles which then get in the way of them taking on more strategic responsibilities.

Saboteurs often play a role in having you hold on to the mindset that you do not have time to grow your people. You block your people's progression and then find that you struggle to retain talent as many move on to better opportunities for stretch, development and progression. You only need to investigate the time cost of losing talent and sourcing, recruiting and developing new hires to see that you should find ways to prioritise developing and nurturing your people.

Learn to share leadership, and you will develop a more committed team, save yourself time, reduce stress and improve productivity. It's not only inclusive – it's smart business!

The threatened leader

In the process of writing this book, I took time out to reflect on my countless coaching sessions with leaders who struggled to let go and share leadership. I also found myself recalling numerous exit interviews

I had conducted with some of the most talented and high-potential employees in client organisations unnecessarily lost to competitors. Those two groups went hand in hand and led to my understanding of why letting go is tough for experienced leaders and ultimately, costly to their organisations. Rife among the comments and feedback from these individuals were comments like:

- 'My progression was stalled because information that was necessary for me to excel in my role was intentionally kept from me.'

- 'My ideas were either ignored or stolen. They often passed these ideas on without giving me credit for them.'

- 'There was zero direction, and no one could tell me what "good" really looks like to them.'

Being an effective leader in the twenty-first century is tough. Many that I have coached to overcome some of the challenges had something in common: they felt threatened. The causes for this were many and varied. Environmental challenges, unhealthy expectations of leadership, and the brilliance and demands of their people fed their insecurities and set off overwhelming alarm bells. Setting my judgements aside, I got curious. It was only then that I got it. They were not bad leaders; they were lost. As I connected more with them and heard their stories, I could empathise. I thought of an empathetic term that would help others to recognise that these leaders were not to blame and the 'threatened leader' was born.

The threatened leader is one that is thrown into this volatile, uncertain, complex and ambiguous (VUCA) world without the necessary support to help them move from the traditional leadership they experienced in their early development years. Without support to unlearn, relearn and reset their leadership, they struggle to cope while needing to appear to know exactly what they are doing. They get defensive when challenged by the more confident, high-potential employees and find themselves in unhealthy cycles that further feed their hidden insecurities. Ultimately, threatened leaders struggle to be inclusive.

Talent threat

Here is an overview of a common relationship between the threatened leader and talent loss. You interview a high-potential candidate or have a career development conversation with a talented team member. You feel excitement at the thought of 'fresh blood' and lots of creativity and ideas kick in. New dreams of possibilities start to emerge – a bit like falling in love for the first time. You think to yourself, 'They have great ideas/talent/whatever skills that my team is needing more of. This is *the* change we need.'

Then the fired-up candidate comes up with ideas. They look at your way of doing things with fresh eyes and their creativity starts to challenge the status quo. This presents a crucial turning point for you as a leader: do you take the saboteur-driven path, or do you choose the path of the leader that knows when to let go?

Every leader comes across key turning points in their leadership journey where they must make a choice between holding on to power or sharing it, and these choices affect how you attract, retain or lose talent. Below is an illustration showing the paths you can take with your talent as they bring new ideas and suggest new ways of doing things within your organisation.

It is normal for experienced leaders to encounter some insecurities as they share leadership. Where not anticipated and tackled, these fears can derail an organisation's development and progression. However, while they never really go away, the fears associated with these insecurities can be effectively managed. Making a conscious decision to brush aside these fears and to ignore the voice of the saboteur will help you to spot and embrace development opportunities.

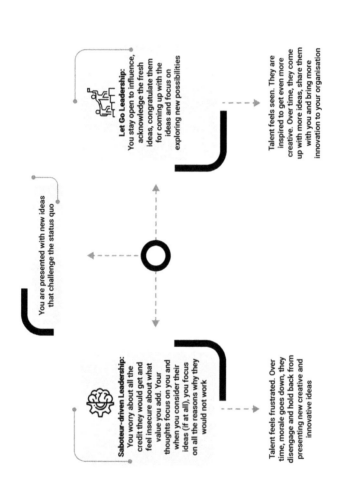

You are presented with new ideas that challenge the status quo

Saboteur-driven Leadership:
You worry about all the credit they would get and feel insecure about what value you add. Your thoughts focus on you and when you consider their ideas (if at all), you focus on all the reasons why they would not work

Let Go Leadership:
You stay open to influence, acknowledge the fresh ideas, congratulate them for coming up with the ideas and focus on exploring new possibilities

Talent feels frustrated. Over time, morale goes down, they disengage and hold back from presenting new creative and innovative ideas

Talent feels seen. They are inspired to get even more creative. Over time, they come up with more ideas, share them with you and bring more innovation to your organisation

Saboteur-driven Leadership vs Let Go Leadership

Imposter syndrome

If you are not familiar with imposter syndrome, it is because it is one of the best-kept secrets in the workplace, present at all levels from job-seeker to CEO.

It has likely kept you up at night as you subconsciously wait for that dreaded phone call that could signal your downfall, or you fret about your talented team member who your saboteur tells you has more to offer the organisation and who is after your job. You probably question whether you have what it takes to lead your team or organisation. Perhaps you put your successes down to luck or fraud and live in fear of being exposed as an imposter. In her book *Lean In: Women, work, and the will to lead,* Sheryl Sandberg beautifully captures the experience of those suffering from imposter syndrome:

> 'Instead of feeling worthy of recognition, they feel undeserving and guilty, as if a mistake has been made. Despite being high achievers, even experts in their fields, women can't seem to shake the sense that it is only a matter of time until they are found out for who they really are – impostors with limited skills or abilities.'[1]

As a female leader, I personally relate to imposter syndrome, both from my years as in-house consultant and now as I run a consultancy business. I have felt this grow stronger the higher up the ladder I rise. While

Sandberg notes imposter syndrome to be particularly prevalent among women, in my experience of coaching senior leaders, I have found imposter syndrome to be just as common among men, although I have found that female leaders find it easier to talk about.

High-performing environment

One of the downsides of being in the company of other high achievers is that you cannot help but compare yourself; this is a great way to feed that imposter syndrome.

In my consultation calls and interviews with senior executives who have achieved tremendous success in their fields, I often find that many are so busy comparing themselves to others that they forget to celebrate their own achievements and recognise their worth. Left unchecked, this can trigger anxiety and feed a level of risk aversion that can stifle creativity. Unmanaged imposter syndrome can be the difference between two high-flyers: one who never quite makes it to the top and the other who smashes through any glass ceiling.

When I reflect on my years in the corporate world, I find it surprising how rarely this common anxiety was voiced by leaders, ironically because of the fear of being exposed as a fraud. In the safety of coaching and on our leadership workshops, where participants can trust that they are among others with shared challenges and experiences, it is heard again and again. On one occasion, a high-profile female banker observed that, once verbalised, 'I realise just how ridiculous and absurd it all sounds. Of course I can be successful!'

If you are in a high-performing environment, the fear of seeming like an imposter and causing others to question your ability can stop you from sharing leadership and empowering those around you. To counter this, ensure that you create spaces where you can share and discuss mistakes with your people, be vulnerable and remember that you are all human.

I once worked with an executive coach client who placed her CEO on a pedestal as the ultimate confident and successful guru. I challenged her to ask him if he ever doubted himself. She reported back that the question led to a closely connected conversation and that his responses had made her realise that he is just as human and fallible as she is.

Take some time to get to know your colleagues better. Ensure that you have peer relationships in which you can openly share experiences – both positive and challenging. Normalise being human to your people to inspire their confidence in their own abilities and potential as leaders.

NUGGETS FOR REFLECTION AND ACTION

Reflect on and journal your responses to the following:

- What thoughts generally come up for you when you consider fully passing on tasks or responsibilities to talented team members?

- Consider your potential successor: do you ever feel threatened by their potential?

- Note down those thoughts and track the feelings that they evoke in you. Think about how they influence the subsequent decisions you make and the extent to which you empower those that are ready for a share in your leadership.

- What excuses do you give for not sharing leadership and what is the resulting cost, to you and to your people?

- What action can you take in the next month to let go and share leadership? What would your saboteur say to hold you back? How will you ensure it doesn't and who could you ask to hold you accountable?

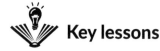 **Key lessons**

By now, you have a sense of what could be getting in the way of you sharing leadership. You have learned that:

- You cannot be inclusive unless you share leadership.

- It is normal to hold on to leadership and, like other leadership skills, the ability to share leadership might have to be learned.

- Saboteurs and imposter syndrome get in the way of inclusive leadership.

- Letting go is not easy, but it is possible.

- High-performing environments can knock your confidence and you are not alone in this.

3
Why You Should Share

N ana shared his screen so that I could see his organisational chart. He introduced each team member's role and with each one, told me why he could not have them take over while he took a month off for much-needed surgery. His coaching sponsor had described how Nana felt strongly that were he to take three or four weeks off work, he could not trust that things would not fall apart in his absence. This time was different though: Nana said that his wife had had enough and that she had threatened to 'rethink their relationship' if he did not start prioritising his health and family.

Six months earlier, Nana had promised his wife that things would change once his new hire, Sarah, settled in and could take some stuff off his plate.

Unfortunately, the ambitious Sarah resigned within five months because, she had explained, 'This was not what I was promised.' Nana was devastated. This was not the first time he had lost talent on which he had placed high hopes. According to him, he could not understand why 'these younger ones do not have patience and are keen to fly before they can walk'.

Nana explained that the CEO seemed to blame him, and recounted a heated conversation in which he had told Nana that if the attrition levels in his division did not improve, they would need to review his role. It seemed that the data from the most recent exit interviews had flagged that people did not feel challenged and stretched enough. The responses from stakeholders who completed a 360-assessment stressed that he needed to identify and work on some leadership challenges – Nana was holding on to power and needed to let go. With compassion and the right support, I had no doubt that Nana could turn things around. I couldn't wait to get started.

Like Nana, in this chapter you will connect with both your personal reasons and the business case for sharing leadership. You will explore why the leadership that got you where you are is not going to get you to the next level. My hope for you is that in the process, you will find a better work-life balance.

The case for sharing

As a leader in today's VUCA world, whether you will ultimately thrive or burn out depends on your willingness to include and engage your people in co-creating your organisational vision, and in finding ways of tackling your business challenges. Shared leadership is a method to step away from many of the challenges, both in the workplace and at home. If you go it alone, you will struggle, your people will disengage and your business will crumble.

However, with so many leaders reluctant to share their vulnerabilities and ask for help, and many organisations still operating with a top-down approach to leadership, it can seem almost impossible to explore other styles of leadership. You might worry that standing apart and becoming an inclusive leader could even be a barrier to staying competitive and achieving greater success. Here is a different perspective: you may not be able to change other leaders' approaches, but by showing up differently, you can influence your team's results and, in doing that, motivate others.

From an organisational perspective, we know that your diversity and inclusion directly influence your success, and that diversity is a key driver of innovation: a 2017 study by the Boston Consulting Group showed that diverse teams produce 19% more revenue.[2] They were able to demonstrate that companies with diverse teams developed more relevant products because their teams had a better understanding of their clients' varied and changing needs.

However, there are also multiple studies that show that *just* being diverse is not enough. One such study by Cloverpop, a company that has built a platform to assist in better business decision-making, found that diversity must be harnessed at every level of decision-making if the business is to get the best out of it. Their study demonstrated that:[3]

- Inclusive teams make better business decisions up to 87% of the time

- Teams that follow an inclusive process make decisions twice as fast with half as many meetings

- Decisions made and executed by diverse teams delivered 60% better results

With those statistics in mind, what gets in the way of harnessing diversity and what can you do about it?

Code-switching

Diversity needs to be present to be harnessed. Leaders either create cultures that allow diversity to thrive or in which it is stifled. In our Safe Space Conversations workshops for diverse, nondominant and often marginalised employee groups, we hear many accounts of employees feeling pressured to stifle their diversity just to 'fit in'. We discuss the concept of 'code-switching', and many are relieved to hear that there is a term for this and that they are not alone. In our workshops, we have found that code-switching is present in all diverse groups (LGBTQIA+, gender, ethnicity, race, mental health, faith, etc), and that in our inclusion work with organisations, the most common form of code-switching that we come across is cultural. According to an article in *Psychology Today*:

'In the broadest sense, code-switching involves adapting the presentation of oneself in ways that disconnect them from the cultural or racial stereotypes of their group. The goal being to enhance the comfort of others, typically those outside of their cultural or racial group, in hopes of receiving equal treatment and opportunities for advancement.'[4]

Research by McKinsey & Company tells us that companies with the most ethnically diverse executive teams are 33% more likely to outperform their peers on profitability,[5] but I wonder how much higher that figure would be if organisations were truly inclusive and diversity wasn't stifled due to systemic pressure to code-switch?

Personally, as a black woman of mixed heritage who has worked in various corporate roles in financial services before setting up my own coaching and consultancy business, code-switching was a key feature of my career journey long before I learned the term. I have had to do a lot of work to recognise that, though successful in those roles, there was so much more I could have offered had I felt safe enough to bring my full self into those environments. I came to see how important it had been for me to 'fit in' in order to be appropriately recognised and rewarded, and how I had therefore learned to marginalise my most diverse parts. As a result of this, these organisations lost a lot of the essence, and ultimately the value, of my diversity. It is fair to say that this acknowledgement drives my mission to create inclusive cultures of shared leadership and empowered relationships where every individual can thrive.

As a leader, actively driving inclusion is your responsibility too. You will need to get to know yourself better, embrace your diversity, bring your own authentic self to work and start to realise the importance of celebrating your own diversity.

As you progress through this book, I will guide you in how to share leadership, creating inclusive environments where your people will not only feel a sense of belonging, but will also find that their diversity is invited, welcomed, appreciated and celebrated. As the research discussed above demonstrates, you will soon come to see the positive impact of this on your organisational performance.

Hybrid world

The Covid-19 pandemic forced new ways of working on organisations and on the world and challenged accepted thinking around the effectiveness of working virtually and flexibly. Many globally dispersed teams were already working in this way but struggled to fit into a business world that favoured colleagues working in shared office locations. Various collaboration and connection tools had of course become available to support virtual working, but the primary focus had always been on building successful workplaces, rather than on successful virtual, flexible workspaces that catered for diverse workstyles and preferences. Flexible working was supported where needed, but never really advocated. Then Covid-19 hit.

Prior to the pandemic, I had already coached several global leadership teams, bringing them together through video conferencing. However, many had resisted virtual team coaching, preferring to come together for offsite meetings, often to the detriment of team members in other locations who were unable to join for a myriad of reasons, or who had to make complex and often expensive travel arrangements.

Of course, in-person sessions remain an important and effective way of bringing teams together and they will always retain a place in a successful business model. Managers and leaders with local teams who have, in the past, been resistant to exploring flexible, virtual and hybrid ways of working, were suddenly forced by the pandemic to review their reasons, as organisations raced to establish new ways of effectively facilitating remote team collaboration. This has, in turn, allowed many businesses to become more inclusive as they prioritise team development events, regardless of member locations, making whatever adjustments are necessary for full participation.

If you are a leader previously determined to monitor your people in the office, you are probably now recognising that this is driven by your own insecurity in leading effectively when you cannot be in the same physical space, or a lack of trust in your people. This self-doubt and the resulting inability to trust that, in your absence, your people are still committed and productive, would have fed the expectation for them to work rigidly from their contracted start time to the end of their day, whether or not this was necessary or a suitable use of their time. The pandemic, and the hybrid world that has emerged from it, has forced leaders to challenge themselves and their established beliefs and principles. It has brought some real progress in terms of increasing inclusivity, but it has also highlighted the importance of creating trusting relationships between you and your people, something that was previously missing in far too many organisations.

Face-time culture

In my time working in both the investment banking and HR divisions of various global financial services organisations, face-time work culture was the norm. Work started early and finished late, and employees were expected to be physically present throughout this time. In one organisation, if you were still working at 9pm, the company would provide both a takeaway meal and a cab from the selection of luxurious, executive car service providers who had contracts with the banks. In my early banking years when I oversaw the recruiting of interns and graduates, these perks were huge selling points, used to attract candidates at career fairs and university presentations. We pulled graduates from the crème de la crème of UK and European universities to join our offices, spoiling them with these daily luxuries as well as visits to expensive bars, outings and periodic sailing trips. We got them in early and had them hooked. I was hooked too!

However, the prestige and lifestyle that came with banking life was at a price: significant face-time expectations and consequently, terrible work-life balance. It remains a price that many are still willing to pay. In 2021, a leaked internal document from Goldman Sachs described overworked junior analysts on the brink of burnout from the workload and stress.[6] Despite today's emphasis on wellbeing and mental health in the workplace, many employees still suffer due to the expectations of their leaders that they will prioritise work over all else. The difference today is that the world expects and demands change. The leaked Goldman Sachs document was greeted with rightful widespread outrage; the current generation entering the workforce is increasingly vocal about mental health challenges, demanding better working conditions and challenging organisational leaders to be, and do, better.

As an inclusive leader required to stay competitive, and retain and nurture talent, you must engage your people in co-creating a healthy, welcoming, flexible and diverse environment where every individual can thrive.

Competition

Many organisations are recognising the growing need to rethink and reset leaders' expectations of their people. A quick browse through the LinkedIn banking jobs listings reveals several companies actively marketing different and creative ways to become more inclusive. Some stress to prospective candidates that they no longer have set expectations regarding 'normal working hours', and others display a direct invitation to returning mothers and candidates from diverse and under-represented groups.

Expectations of current and future employee populations have changed, so organisations are having to adapt and accommodate, or they will lose out. These expectations require that as a leader, you share leadership. Leading as you were led, or as you feel most comfortable leading, and expecting that your people will follow, will no longer get you or your organisation far. To stay ahead in a fast-moving competition, you need to work with your people to co-create inclusive environments where diversity is welcomed and nurtured.

Groupthink

Perhaps the most important reason for you to become an inclusive leader is that we know that diversity adds value to your organisation. To grow leaders that will take your organisation to the next level, you must be inclusive yourself.

I recently challenged a leader whose executive team was made up of predominantly white, male and experienced leaders. When I questioned this, he stated that it was unavoidable. To explore this, we spent some time reviewing their company website, their LinkedIn posts and their job descriptions, and we both saw how each one could have been written by the same person. I explained that if I were a prospective female, black candidate, just a quick glance at the photograph on their website team page would trigger some anxiety in me and make me question whether this was a company in which I would feel truly welcome. What if

I was a woman going through menopause, or from the LGBTQIA+ community, or from any other non-dominant group? I encouraged him to consider an even wider range of diverse, potential new employees with differences: how would each of these receive the company profile or the focus on their communication and marketing efforts? I invited him to be more compassionate and empathetic, listening to and learning from his employees, both current and potential, and to practise being less defensive. It was then that he got it.

We underwent a process of exploring each of his current executive team members in turn. Now willing to explore how each had obtained their positions, he described how many had landed their roles through personal recommendations, references and introductions from a small, privileged circle. Reliance on drawing from such a small candidate pool ensures little or no diversity and sets up additional challenges for those coming in from outside. Recognising this kicked off his work on diversifying his network, the resources he relied on and the lens through which he looked at the world.

Perhaps you already have a diverse team? By now, you will hopefully recognise that that does not mean you are inclusive. If you lead an organisation that is not inclusive, it does not matter how diverse your people are, groupthink will become the norm. According to *Psychology Today*, 'Groupthink is a phenomenon that occurs when a group of well-intentioned people makes irrational or nonoptimal decisions spurred by the urge to conform or the belief that dissent is impossible.'[7]

If, as a black African woman, I must show up and act as though I were a white man, marginalising my differences that were shaped by my African upbringing to 'fit in', what value does my diversity add to your organisation – beyond making your data look better perhaps? If the diversity of your team or organisation does not in any way shape the culture and influence the decisions you make as an organisation, then what is the point?

 NUGGETS FOR REFLECTION AND ACTION

Reflect on and journal your responses to the following:

- How diverse is your organisation?
- Looking in from outside, based on what they would see, hear and read, are there specific groups of people that would be attracted because they would feel a better sense of belonging in your organisation?
- Is there an equity of power in voices within your organisation?
- If not, are you using your privileges in the service of those with less power?
- Is it your voice that gets heard the most? Do your people feel safe enough and are they empowered to challenge your thinking?

- Has your diversity shaped your decisions and organisational direction?
- If I were to walk into your organisation or meet your team, would the culture reflect the diversity of your people, or is it a reflection of you as the leader?
- Will you ask your people to reflect on the above questions with you? How about inviting them to join you in co-creating the right culture for all?

Harnessing diversity

A friend of mine recently shared an article on *Yahoo! Finance* about research commissioned by the file-sharing company WeTransfer that, 'suggests that brainstorming is a giant waste of time'.[8] Based on a 2019 survey of 20,000 creative professionals from 197 countries, it identified that the majority found brainstorming to be 'largely unhelpful for solving a creative challenge.' In response, WeTransfer's then CEO, Rob Alderson, observed that, 'In the creative world we hear an awful lot about collaboration, but it seems that while working together is essential to bring an idea to life, it's not that good for shaping ideas in the first place.'

I disagree.

When I look at the results of the research through an inclusion lens, I find that it illustrates the need for leaders to be coached and developed to become inclusive.[9] When we challenge thinking around inclusion in organisations, this is one of the blind spots that often comes up. Just bringing a diverse group of people together does not automatically mean that you are inclusive and able to harness the diversity that you have. Renowned diversity advocate Verna Myers says that 'diversity is being invited to the party; inclusion is being asked to dance.'[10] I will take this further by adding that just being asked to dance is not enough. My responses would be:

- Is the music right for me?

- Do I know how to dance to the tunes you are playing?

- If I have been raised without your privileges, do I need some support to build the confidence to dance the way that I feel most comfortable dancing, knowing that my style is different and that it will be more noticeable if/when I trip?

- What if I introduced my own music and ways of dancing and we co-created new tunes and dance moves?

Where leadership is not shared, diversity can be introduced but if leadership is still held on to by a select group of individuals, it will inadvertently feed a culture that expects and thrives on conformity. You will only be able to harness the value of diverse thinking when you create a safe space, one in which the leaders are willing to step aside, challenge their own biases, build trust and create safe environments where everyone feels able to speak up, without fear of damaging relationships or making career-limiting mistakes.

Harnessing diversity is not easy. It is a journey that requires that you engage with different perspectives in figuring out how best to do this in your organisation. In the process, it is important that you take care of yourself and your people as you make changes.

Stress & burnout

To survive and thrive in today's VUCA world, you need to take care of yourself as a leader. Stress and burnout will feature regularly in your life if you do not share leadership. A stressed leader creates stressful workspaces.

The figures are striking. Kronos Incorporated and the Future Workplace research firm conducted a study as part of their 2016 Employee Engagement Lifecycle Series and found that 95% of human resource leaders admit employee burnout is sabotaging workforce retention.[11] Harvard Business School estimates that stress-related burnout may impose a healthcare cost of $125 to $190 billion a year in the US alone.[12]

Maslach and Leiter for the journal *World Psychiatry* describe burnout as 'a psychological syndrome emerging as a prolonged response to chronic interpersonal stressors on the job.'[13] They note three dimensions that characterise burnout:

1. Feelings of overwhelming exhaustion or energy depletion

2. Increased feelings of cynicism or mental detachment from one's job

3. A sense of ineffectiveness and lack of accomplishment

Each of these dimensions can be influenced by your leadership, the extent to which you take care of your people and whether they feel appreciated and included within your team or organisation.

Prospective clients who approach me for inclusive leadership coaching have either themselves chosen to reach out for support (often later than they should have done), or they may have been referred for coaching by their organisations who may recognise that they are on the cusp of a breakdown. All too often, our initial consultation reveals strong indicators of burnout syndrome. Many have found work taking over their lives and struggle to even imagine a healthier balance. We often find that stress and burnout already feature heavily in their organisational cultures, alongside the high levels of sickness absences, absenteeism and attrition that result.

As a leader, you need to take care of yourself and model prioritising your wellbeing. You also need to ensure that your people are taken care of. High levels of stress and burnout signal that expectation management is ineffective and rectifying this must be prioritised. Coaching just one or two individuals on how to manage stress is short-sighted and ignores the systemic causes behind such issues. It is like putting a plaster on a bleeding bullet wound, without first addressing the true source of the blood.

 NUGGETS FOR REFLECTION AND ACTION

Reflect on and journal your responses to the following:

- Where in your team is work needed to ensure that both individual and collective wellbeing is better taken care of?
- What is your role in that process?
- To what extent do you model a healthy work-life balance? How good are your boundaries on time? How do you protect your time with your family, fitness, fun and/or other outside activities?
- What would a culture that advocates a healthy work-life balance look like, and where is change needed in your organisation?
- For the sake of your own wellbeing and their development, how can you share leadership of that change journey with your people rather than take it on as your sole responsibility?

Values

Fulfilment in life comes from honouring and living our values. As you live your day-to-day life, you will come to recognise your own particular set of values as you experience a particular sense of achievement or pride in your work, or when you feel particularly triggered by an event. Understanding that we each hold different sets of values explains why one person might have a totally different reaction to the same event than another. Your values are key to understanding what matters to you. There are values that make you jump out of bed in the morning, drive your behaviours throughout the day and help you choose one course of action over another.

A lot has been said and written about values over the years. Too often individuals and companies throw out a list of words which they claim to be their values but without having taken the time to truly assess and establish what they really mean to them, what they would look like if practised in their daily lives, and the impact of not honouring those values.

Prior to leaving my role as a vice president in financial services, I spent a significant amount of time analysing which parts of my work brought me joy and would become non-negotiable when considering my next steps. I tracked what I did for a couple of months and allocated a 'spark factor' to each activity, and then at the end of that exercise I sat down to identify the top five values that kept me buzzing at work:

1. Service

2. Fairness and justice

3. Respect

4. Connection

5. Freedom

Understanding my own values helped me decide to leave a role after an organisational change. It had been easy to refuse the revised job offered to me because I knew that it would no longer align with my values. Without sufficient value alignment, the job would have restricted my freedom and creativity without offering me sufficient fulfilment. Clarity around my values helped me narrow down career options and led me to the work I do today, work that brings me huge fulfilment by honouring my core values and more!

Understanding your values and those of your team members will be key to how inclusive you become as a leader. It is important that you think through the values that make you who you are and consider how you will keep those alive in your leadership, especially as you begin to share leadership more. Only through this process of self-discovery will you come to be authentic in your leadership and connect with your people in a way that also permits them to bring their full and varied selves to work, enabling you to harness your diversity and build collective engagement. Being clear on your values helps you make the right decisions, influences the vision you have for your organisation and informs the culture that you all help to shape.

A common mistake that leaders make is to assume that everyone is equally motivated by status like job titles, financial reward or promotions. Taking time to get to know your people will provide guidance on how best to motivate them, and make them feel welcomed and valued.

 NUGGETS FOR REFLECTION AND ACTION

Reflect on and journal your responses to the following:

- What are your top five values? List and highlight them in your notebook as you will be invited to refer back to them in Chapter Four.

- Think of the last time you felt truly angry at a situation or person and consider the cause of this anger. Could it have been because one of your top values was being undermined? Which value was it?

- Which values drive who you are as a leader?

- How about your team members? Have you had conversations with each one to help you understand their top values?

- If not, why not? If you have, to what extent have you aligned their current responsibilities to those values?

- Could you, as their leader, ask your team members to identify their own top values? Note how closely your assessment of their values and their own understanding align. If there are significant differences, together explore why.
- How do you, as their leader, facilitate that alignment between their values and responsibility to ensure maximal career fulfilment and employee engagement?

Legacy

Your legacy as a leader will be determined by the leadership decisions you make and how closely they align with your values. A successful legacy is driven by how well you serve and grow your people.

Having had the privilege of both working with and coaching leaders from across various organisations, industries and continents, I have observed just how strongly leaders impact their people and organisations, while they are part of them and even after they have left. How inclusive you are as a leader will influence the legacy you leave behind: who will remember you and what you will be remembered for.

When I bring up the notion of legacy with the leaders I coach, I often find that they are so focused on the establishment and protection of their current reputation and the avoidance of anything that could risk that reputation that they have given little thought to their future legacy. Research supporting this suggests that it is common for leaders to focus almost exclusively on the avoidance of negative legacies, rather than on the proactive generation of a positive legacy to leave behind.[14] Sometimes only the thought of death would be enough to force the focus on creating a positive legacy.

Consider Alfred Nobel (1833–1896), a Swedish chemist and engineer now best known for establishing the Nobel Prize awards.[15] As a scientist, his most important invention was dynamite, an explosive soon in use worldwide for mining and other civilian structural explosions, but later transforming warfare. In 1888, after the death of Ludvig Nobel, Alfred's brother, several French newspapers mistakenly published obituaries for the wrong brother. One newspaper headline confidently proclaimed '*Le marchand de la mort est mort*' ('The merchant of death is dead'). A pacifist, Alfred Nobel is said to have been so horrified that his legacy was to be as 'the merchant of death' that he went on to bequeath a significant portion of his vast fortune to creating the Nobel Prize awards to recognise those who 'have conferred the greatest benefit on mankind', which have since become his legacy.[16]

Here's another exemplary and recent display of legacy, and one of the most inspiring leadership legacies I've come across in recent years. Jamal Edwards, a black British icon who died at the age of thirty-one in 2022 was a legend. From his teenage years he was dedicated to raising the profile of music artists that were not being represented by mainstream media and went on to create SBTV, a platform that has been credited for launching the careers of some of the UK's biggest artists. He was also an ambassador for the Prince's Trust, a UK charity that supports eleven to thirty-year-olds who are unemployed or at risk of exclusion from school.[17]

When the news of his death came out, there was a huge outpouring of condolences, and stories of love and his impact as a friend, leader, mentor and inspiration from thousands of people whose lives he had touched and shaped in mind-blowing ways. Stories were shared of how he met talented artists on the streets, gave them his full attention, made them feel seen, heard and celebrated, then went ahead to facilitate the launch of their successful music careers. It was clear that this was a man who was present in his relationships and made a difference in his short time on earth.

People will remember you for how you made them feel. As an inclusive leader, you are living out your legacy today – both in your personal and professional life. You do not have to wait until the end of your time with your people or your organisation before you start thinking about how you will be remembered.

In coaching, I often get my clients to create a vision for the legacy they wish to leave. We then look at the gaps between their current leadership and their desired leadership legacy and start to come up with ways to bridge that gap.

Making your people feel included and empowered today is the starting point to living your positive legacy. By the end of this book, you will know exactly how to do that.

 NUGGETS FOR REFLECTION AND ACTION

Reflect on and journal your responses to the following:

- What story would you want your people to tell of your leadership impact and legacy?
- Where would you place yourself along the journey to creating a legacy that you would be proud of? You may choose to consider your progress along this journey on a scale of 1–10 so you can later quantify your progress.
- Whatever your score, reflect on what 9/10 would look like? What would 10/10 look like? What steps could you take to get you there, and for accountability, who could you share that goal with?

 **Key lessons**

Following this chapter, you now have a better sense of the need for inclusive leadership in today's world. You have learned that:

- The approach to leadership that got us here will hold us here and prevent progress.

- To stay competitive and to ensure your organisation's survival in today's VUCA world, you need to share leadership.

- For your own wellbeing and to meet the demands of leadership, you need to be inclusive.

- Before you can share leadership, you need to understand your own values so you can be authentic as a leader.

- Your legacy is one to start shaping and living today, not to be left until after you are gone.

4
Get Ready To Share

'I know what he's going to say. He has already said it several times... He trusts me and wants me to take over from him eventually, but he doesn't feel like I'm ready yet.' Amal and I were getting ready for our three-way meeting with his boss, Leo.

This was my second meeting with Amal, a new executive coaching client being sponsored by his organisation. He was on the succession plan to take over from their audit department head, Leo, but the organisation felt that Amal was not yet quite ready and needed another eighteen months.

As part of the 'Seek Feedback' and 'Have Accountability' phases (to be introduced in the next chapters) of onboarding new executive coaching clients, I meet with both the client and their coaching sponsor (often their boss). The meeting is designed to ensure alignment on the coaching goals, and more importantly, to stress to the sponsor that our coaching engagement is confidential and that it is up to my client (in this case, Amal) to choose how much of the coaching they are willing to share. I never share information directly with the sponsor, thus ensuring that my client and I can create a truly confidential, safe and trusting relationship for our work together. (The only exceptions to this are any conditions under which information should not be kept confidential in accordance with the International Coach Federation's ethical standards, for example, if someone discloses illegal activity, if I'm required to do so by a court order or subpoena, if there is imminent or likely risk of danger to self or to others, etc.[18])

Leo's name and face appeared on the screen and I saw Amal's face tighten. He was nervous and I wasn't surprised. Earlier in the year, Amal had been disappointed when he was turned down for a promotion. After several conversations with Leo, including one in which Amal had complained that he had been treated unfairly, they had decided that some coaching would help him to understand why the organisation felt that he wasn't yet ready and to prepare him to lead a bigger team. Leo was getting ready to step down and move on from banking. He was nearing retirement and wanted to spend more time with his grandson who had received a recent health diagnosis. He had already mentioned his retirement plan to HR and Leo was keen to be freed up to support his daughter as she prepared to return to work after a long maternity leave.

Amal had already attended several leadership training programmes and seemed to know all the right things, yet Leo insisted that Amal was not getting the best out of his team and did not set a good example because he always seemed so stretched. In our first meeting, Amal admitted that he needed to build his confidence; not only did he fall into the problem solver archetype, but he was also a perfectionist. He confessed that he was having problems at home because his family often complained that all he did was work, think about or talk about work. If Amal did not sort out his work-life balance, he would lose out both at work and at home. He was out of ideas and needed to understand how to tackle the ever-increasing demands of his role while also freeing up more time for his family.

I assured him that this challenge was not uncommon and that I believed that, through coaching, he could achieve the balance he craved. The secret was in leading his team differently and empowering them so he could get the best out of them. First, though, we needed to get Amal ready to share leadership, then coach him to walk his team through our SHARE Leadership journey. As Amal progressed through his coaching journey, we recognised that holding on to leadership was Amal's comfort zone, a common reason for leaders not sharing.

From comfort to stretch

Through all areas of life, we establish our personal comfort zones. When we look back, we find that our tendencies to stay within these familiar areas are often influenced by the role models we had growing up. People often talk about being inspired by their teachers, parents and key carers from their formative years. To get to where I am today, I have made several life-changing decisions: to move countries because the course I wanted to study was not offered in English in Finland where I lived at the time, to leave my corporate role and set up my own business, to end my marriage and take charge of my family's security and fulfilment. On each occasion I had consciously brought certain role models to mind as though to prove to myself that I could make it work. Each time I had engaged in a mind battle between thoughts of possible doom, representing the voice of the saboteur determined to keep me in my comfort zone, and those of liberation championing my ability to create greater fulfilment and success. Change is tough, but it can be worthwhile. As a leader who has decided to become inclusive, you will fight similar battles every day.

In leadership, it is easy to find yourself holding on tightly to the roles and responsibilities that lie within your comfort zone. This does not just limit you but will also hold your team back. This tendency to remain within your comfort zone is the reason why there are so many blockers in leadership positions holding their people and organisations back. It also explains why talented employees become frustrated and leave, as blockers get in the way of them bringing their wisdom, creativity and innovation to play in the workplace. In 2019, the HRDIRECTOR website published an article reporting on the results of the annual UK Reward Management Survey conducted by Paydata, a reward management consultancy firm.[19] The results exposed some real concerns for the next twelve months: of the HR directors who entered the survey, 66% expected to experience recruitment difficulties, and 62% were anticipating retention issues, an increase from 40% the previous year. As coaches, my colleagues and I are finding that leaders are feeling growing pressure to engage and positively challenge their workforce as competition for talent is increasingly fierce and retention difficulties grow.

Traditional leaders struggle the most as they fight to hold on to power in an environment that requires letting go and sharing power. It doesn't have to be that way. In your quest to become inclusive you need to move away from being the expert and lean into your people more. Your saboteur might push you to stay within your comfort zone, but by recognising this you will be empowered to fight back, step back and develop a stronger relationship with your stretch zone.

Stretch zone

Your stretch zone is that area beyond your comfort zone where discomfort and uncertainty kick in; it is also an area where possibilities are endless and real change can happen. We have comfort and stretch zones across all areas of our lives: in finance, relationship, career, etc. Learning to identify your default position when it comes to various situations will help you understand when to push yourself to step back and leave space for both yourself and others, and when you need to move into your stretch zone. As an inclusive leader, your role is also to help your people to recognise their comfort vs stretch zones too.

There will often be a gap between your comfort zone and your stretch zone; identifying this gap will reveal your development needs. If you do not constantly explore and challenge these gaps, you will restrict your people's development and become a blocker. You will also stifle your organisation's growth and prevent it from staying competitive and relevant. One way to protect against this is to make sure you keep your people dreaming. Everyone needs to be clear on your vision and on the role they each play in getting your organisation to where it wants to be. When you joined as a leader, you probably had a vision of where you wanted to take your organisation. You may have managed to keep that vision alive in your leadership or it may have fallen by the wayside. In either case, it is important that you reflect on your earlier vision before then sharing it with your people so that you can collectively co-create and align around a shared vision for your organisation. Let's start with your personal vision for your leadership.

Leadership vision

If you were made redundant next week but also presented with an opportunity to take over a new organisation, leading it in a way that is different, with no constraints or barriers in the way, how would you choose to shape its culture? Who would you be as a leader? How would you like your people to describe your leadership? Dream, dream, dream!

To dream is about visualising and preparing to make way for new realities. I often facilitate visioning exercises with leaders on our development programmes. For some leaders, this is the first time they have taken time to come up with a compelling vision for their work as leaders. It can sometimes be an emotional exercise for leaders as they come to realise the potential that they have to make a significant impact on their people and their organisations. Too often I find that the ongoing demands and pressures of leadership has meant that the time and space required to effectively explore that leadership vision has never been prioritised.

I recently reviewed some work I had done with a client on a leadership development coaching programme. Our first few months were spent exploring and working on their own self-limiting beliefs, but about halfway through their programme, I felt that they were ready to put these aside and I had suggested that we go wild with the dreaming process. We spent some time separately imagining and outlining our best dreams and visions for this client; I knew them quite well by this stage and my vision for them was exciting and ambitious. We then compared our visions, noting with fascination how similar our dreams for them were, before combining and setting aside the big dream vision and continuing through their development programme. About six months later, I pulled out the big dream vision for them to review and they were astounded! In their own words, 'Goodness, that's totally me. I've become all that and more.'

As a result of dreaming and then verbalising their dreams, they had become more tangible. Over time, they started the process of working out how to make them a reality. They had found that, by keeping this vision at the forefront of their mind, they had started to identify and explore opportunities that they would previously have ignored.

One of my favourite quotes is a couple of lines from a loose translation of a few lines from Johann Wolfgang von Goethe's tragic play *Faust*:

Whatever you can do, or dream you can, begin it.
Boldness has genius, power, and magic in it![20]

This famous quotation brilliantly encapsulates the importance of taking time to dream and opening yourself up to new possibilities. The more you do that, the sooner you can begin the journey of making your dreams a reality. As with my coaching client, your own limiting beliefs could be holding you back and keeping you unfulfilled.

As a leader, if you do not dream and allow yourself to explore the endless and wonderful possibilities offered by the future, letting go and empowering others to lead will feel more like a threat than an opportunity for you to explore new paths. You will hold on to the responsibilities that lie within your comfort zone and you will be keeping your saboteur happy by playing small. Allowing yourself to dream – and to dream big – will stretch not only you but your organisation to greater heights.

 NUGGETS FOR REFLECTION AND ACTION

Reflect on and journal your responses to the following:

- What is your vision for your organisation?
- As a leader, where would you like to take your organisation?
- What possibilities lie ahead for you personally?

- Can you identify any dreams that could be getting shut down or blocked by your saboteur? If so, how will you mitigate the risk so you move ahead?
- What vision do you need to verbalise so you can work towards making it a reality?
- How will you verbalise this vision and to whom?

Unleash diversity

As you reflect on your leadership vision and who you need to be to achieve it, your insecurities are bound to show up. Expecting them and recognising that they are driven by your saboteur will ensure that they do not get in your way, or stand in the way of you giving yourself permission to show up fully and authentically in your leadership.

As you start to expose the negative thoughts and beliefs you hear in the voice of your saboteur, you will come to see that not only do these negative elements hold you back and keep you small, but they may have forced you to marginalise some aspects of yourself that make you unique. If I take myself as an example, it wasn't until I set up my own business and stopped trying to fit in to a world created by and structured around others that I realised that my diversity was my power.

I was born to a Finnish mother and Nigerian father in Germany, where they were both studying medicine.

After my parents qualified in the early 1980s, we moved back to Nigeria, where they set up their private hospital in the southern town of Awka. My siblings and I grew up within the hospital premises, attended the local primary schools and went on to boarding schools in other cities as we got older. I moved to Finland in my late teens and then to London in my early twenties. My experiences growing up, particularly those from my childhood in Nigeria, heavily influenced the person I became as I grew up, and indeed, who I am today.

I have a rich cultural heritage. The cultures of Nigeria and Finland could not be more different. Then the culture in the UK was added to the mix. When I entered the British workplace, I found myself working tirelessly to make myself fit in and to appear as 'British' as possible. Only later, when I really started exploring myself and identifying my core values, did I come to understand that, in trying to fit in, I had marginalised those parts of myself that fed my self-love, creativity and confidence. Embracing and celebrating those and other differences has enabled me to channel them into the work I do now with organisations. My diversity has become my unique selling point.

As an inclusive leader, you also need to undertake that journey of self-discovery before you can lead others on it and coach them to bring the value of their diversity into your organisation.

NUGGETS FOR REFLECTION AND ACTION

Reflect on and journal your responses to the following:

- Go back to the values you highlighted in your notebook, and reflect on how your experiences have informed those values. Which of those values do you manifest more strongly outside of work than within?

- Think of a work situation where you hold back. What is your public stance on that situation? Is this truly authentic, or is there a 'hidden stance' that you do not share? How does your upbringing or other socialisation influence your position and behaviour here?

- What makes you keep that part of you hidden? What judgements are you making or assuming others will make?

- What is the impact on you of not showing up fully and authentically at work?

- What might happen if you felt able to do so more? Could it give others permission to do the same?

When you put energy into trying to be who you are not, you create stress for yourself. In small doses, that is understandable. Over extended periods of time, that becomes a real challenge and can start to affect your mental health. The more you bring your full self into your work and leadership, the more you empower and inspire your people to do the same. That is inclusive leadership.

Self-care and compassion

If you find yourself complaining about anxiety, inability to focus and a feeling of overwhelm, these are all signs that you may be suffering from stress. In her research and work on self-compassion, Dr Kristin Neff, an associate professor of educational psychology at the University of Texas, identifies self-compassion as having three component paradigms:[21]

1. **'Self-kindness vs self-judgement':** This is self-explanatory as the quality of being kind to yourself rather than always criticising and judging, particularly in times of additional stress or struggle. This drive to self-criticise is often driven by your saboteur, but learning to recognise this and tackle it will help you de-escalate stress.

2. **'Common humanity vs isolation':** This involves recognising that, like all humans, you are imperfect. Self-compassion involves accepting this and understanding that, like everyone, there will be times when you will trip up and make mistakes, but that you can also give yourself permission to acknowledge these mistakes and still get up, dust yourself off and try again.

3. **'Mindfulness vs over-identification':** This involves maintaining a fair balance between our positive and negative emotions. Negative emotions can be accepted, not judged, supressed or denied, but must also be considered in relation

to the larger perspective of ourselves and others. To avoid overwhelm, ensure that these negative emotions are held, but only to a proportionate and measured degree.

All three elements lie well within your capabilities, but showing self-compassion, like all new skills, will require practice, practice and more practice! All through life, we have acquired new skills and then practised them so consistently that they have turned into habits; consider how you can wash your hands without going through every step of the process, or how you drive to work or to the train station without focusing on every step. Activities that we have mastered become those that we can perform on 'auto-pilot'; the same goes for our thoughts. Consistent practice does indeed make perfect. Understanding how this leads to the development of new and better habits will, in turn, serve as a reminder to prioritise this practice.

The art of demonstrating self-compassion through the practice of self-kindness – normalising and accepting that you are an imperfect human – and mindfulness is also a skill that, with practice, can become a habit. These habits will strengthen your ability to let go of leading from the front and remind you of the power of developing leadership in others, without beating yourself up in the process. Repetition of these habits will so ingrain them within your thoughts that self-compassion will become automatic, no longer requiring additional effort, and always available to you, particularly when most needed in times of additional stress.

Inclusive leadership is not easy work. I would like you to consider mindfulness in more detail, particularly if it is a new practice for you to learn.

Be mindful

Years ago, when I trained with the British Mindfulness Institute and subsequently the NeuroLeadership Institute, we were taught that mindfulness can result in structural changes in our brains. This is backed by research which has shown that meditation 'may be associated with structural changes in areas of the brain that are important for sensory, cognitive and emotional processing',[22] and means meditation could help us build our capacity to control our impulsive emotional reactions and help us stay calm under pressure.

Within the prefrontal cortex of the brain there is a small area considered to be the brain's braking system – the ventrolateral prefrontal cortex. It plays a vital role in allowing us to focus by inhibiting environmental distractions when needed and may also help in reducing the feeling of overwhelm. Unfortunately, the location of the braking area within the energy-hungry prefrontal cortex means that it runs out of energy quickly and its efficiency diminishes over time and with use. Being mindful will help you recognise when your brain and body call for a break. These periods are needed to allow your brain to rest, recover and function better. With constant stress and no downtime, it is no surprise that the brain moves to protect itself, introducing its own downtime and can even feel like it has shut down, as can be seen in executives suffering from burnout.

I often have new clients frown at the suggestion that one of the practices they need more of is mindfulness, frequently asking, 'Who has time to meditate?' Contrary to many assumptions, mindfulness practice does not require that you block out periods of time in your already busy schedule specifically to meditate. You can be a strong mindfulness practitioner by incorporating mindfulness into your day-to-day activities.

I have had executive coaching clients rush into our meetings frazzled and unable to think. There are times when I have had to kick off sessions with short mindfulness activities just to let them become present enough to be able to think and engage in the coaching session.

My first main introduction to mindfulness was through an eight-week mindfulness-based stress reduction programme run in a local wellness clinic near my home in East Dulwich, in London.[23] I remember wondering at the time how my now ex-husband

and I would have the energy or time to head off to a mindfulness workshop after a long, hard day at work and an evening getting our little ones to bed. Yet we made the commitment, and to ensure there was no turning back, booked our babysitter for all the dates. By the end of the eight sessions, it was clear that the programme had been a worthwhile investment of time and effort. With a better understanding of me, my triggers and thought processes, I was able to redirect thoughts that would, if left unchecked, have led to stress. I slept better. I was more present in my day-to-day activities and life felt calmer. It was this appreciation of mindfulness and its impact that influenced my decision to undertake further studies with the British Mindfulness Institute.

During one of our mindfulness training sessions, we were sent out to take a mindful walk around the busy streets of Kings Cross in London. Committed to being totally present, I wandered around the hectic and bustling streets, then moved on to a nearby park to continue my walk. I paid attention to, and really noticed, the physical sensations of walking, the contact my feet made with the ground with each step, the tiny movement of my toes, ankles, knees and arms, the feeling of the fabric of my clothes against my skin, the sounds, the smells, the burst of colours all around me. There was no space to think about anything else but the intensity of using all my senses and consequent feeling of being truly alive. The experience was mind-blowing, and I felt so liberated!

In their book, *Mindfulness: A practical guide to finding peace in a frantic world*,[24] Mark Williams and Dr Danny Penman tell us that through the space and time that mindfulness offers, we become better able to choose the best solution to our problems. That has indeed been my experience. As an inclusive leader, practising mindful living will help you make the most of these growth possibilities, developing that part of your brain that will allow you to be fully present with your people. To do so, you need to slow down to witness and harness the diversity in your people, and to create safe spaces for them to show up fully. Being mindful and present is one of the toughest challenges that my busy clients face as they transform themselves to become more inclusive. It takes practice and commitment to being more and doing less – both in the service of inclusion.

Embrace being

At one event, a participant asked my plans for the rest of the day and I proudly explained that I planned 'to do nothing!' She smiled and said, 'That would be *niksen* then.' Intrigued by our brief chat, I did some research and learned that this Dutch concept beautifully describes what I often recommend to my clients as 'just being' time. The difference between mindfulness and *niksen* is that unlike mindfulness, *niksen* advocates just being, without a need to pay attention to where your mind is going and directing it back to the present moment.[25] If, like me, you grew up in communities where doing nothing was considered lazy, this one will mess with your brain, and you will have some unlearning to do!

I can link the concept of *niksen* both to my neuroscience studies and my own experience. Both have taught me that when we are calm, our thinking is calm, enabling us to come up with creative ideas and to make better choices. Have you noticed how you come up with great ideas in those moments when you're relaxed on a sofa doing nothing, in the shower or when you settle into bed at night and relax? I now keep a notebook by my bedside so I can capture those 'gold dust' ideas and get straight back to enjoying doing nothing.

We all need downtime in our busy, hectic lives and just like mindfulness, we need to learn to embrace it as positive *niksen* time, rich with potential and possibilities. Learning to give your brain a well-earned break may effortlessly, and often quite enjoyably, improve your creativity, productivity and even innovation.

 **Key lessons**

To let go and share leadership is not easy, but it is key to our survival as leaders and organisations. As you grow as an inclusive leader, remember that:

- Your ability to problem-solve and get things done has probably played a key role in getting you to where you are today.

- The leadership you experienced in the past probably favoured 'calling the shots' as a leader, not sharing leadership.

- Self-care is important on this journey and you need to be kind to yourself as you navigate and grow as an inclusive leader.

- Your pace as a leader will influence how effective you can be as an inclusive leader.

- Inclusion is a journey, not a destination. As an inclusive leader, you must keep growing your self-awareness, learning about differences and engaging your people in your own development.

In the next chapter, you will be introduced to our SHARE Leadership model. With clarity on your archetype and tendencies, you will come to further understand the underlying dynamics that they influence and learn practical solutions to ensure that you maximise your potential as an inclusive leader.

PART TWO
SHARE LEADERSHIP

The first part of this book focused on the work that you need to do on self-leadership to be able to let go and lay solid foundations that will enable you to share power as you become an inclusive leader.

Part Two describes how you must prepare your team(s) to lead with you. It will guide you through the developmental areas that emerge for our clients as they work through our SHARE Leadership approach, and more importantly, what awareness and changes they must make to become more inclusive. Be sure to review all the exercises from Part One before moving on to Part Two, as they were designed to leave you ready to tackle the following sections, gradually preparing you to become inclusive. My hope is that by the end of this second part of the book you will feel better equipped to get the best out of your people.

Our unique SHARE Leadership method is based on the principle that for organisations to get the best out of their people, leadership should be distributed among everyone. This easy-to-apply model focuses on the pooling of all resources available to an organisation for maximum effectiveness, regardless of where they sit in the hierarchy. Whether you are on the board, the CEO, a senior leader, a manager, have just joined a company, or are an entrepreneur, our SHARE Leadership method will equip you with the skills and tools you need to maximise the collective potential of your people and organisation.

I developed our SHARE Leadership method based on experience gained through our successful leadership and team coaching programme, coupled with the various tried-and-tested techniques we employ to ensure that our clients complete our programmes without developing a dependency on us. We are committed to leaving our clients empowered to drive and sustain the positive changes that we cultivate and facilitate within their organisations. We have also observed that leaders and organisations that go on to adopt the same approach when working with their teams can create inclusive cultures driven by shared leadership and transformed relationships, both within their organisations and with their stakeholders.

To ensure that I captured the key challenges that leaders are presented with in today's workplace, I analysed the feedback obtained from our many years of running our leadership development programmes, and I combined this with lessons learned through my own experiences in and of leadership, and from my work with hundreds of leaders across various organisations, sectors and countries. It became clear that most of the challenges that stood in the way of inclusive and high-performing leadership could be addressed by focusing on five key areas. This led to the development of our SHARE Leadership method which now underpins each of our leadership, team and organisational development programmes.

The inclusive leader consistently walks each step of our SHARE Leadership model: they **S**eek feedback, **H**ave accountability, **A**dapt regularly, **R**econnect with their people as they all stretch and **E**mpower their people. The circular nature of the model highlights that sharing leadership is a continuous process and is never completed.

5

S – Seek Feedback

If you have a culture of feedback, there will be mutual support and trust in your teams and team members will look out for one another. You will all view mistakes as opportunities for learning and development. Inclusive leaders share leadership and shape cultures of co-creation by regularly seeking feedback. If you are a leader that regularly seeks feedback, you will shape an organisation that understands the value of feedback – giving, seeking, receiving and growing from it. Otherwise, how else would you know if your intentions do not match your impact?

In this chapter, you will build your self-awareness, reflect on your relationship with others and learn more about your impact. You will start to step into the shoes of others, build empathy and identify learning opportunities as you grow into becoming fairer and more inclusive in your leadership.

Glenn was the CEO of a financial services company that had scaled rapidly. Following months of rolling out a new initiative, he had asked his team members if they felt included in his decision-making and looked from one team member to another. Without even answering the question, their facial expressions told him everything he needed to know: he had moved ahead with the initiative without checking that his people were truly with him.

I had met Glenn at a networking event a couple of years before the company's growth and he had been fascinated by the systemic approach of my coaching work. We had agreed to stay connected via LinkedIn and he had said that he believed his company would benefit from our services at some point. Glenn had stayed engaged in the content I regularly shared on the platform and had periodically sent private messages about posts that had most resonated with him, but I hadn't really expected him to follow up about my services, so I was surprised to receive an email from him asking to discuss some of the challenges he was having with his leadership team.

Glenn was clearly well respected, and from the way he spoke about his people, it was clear that he was a good leader who wanted their workplace to be welcoming and their careers fulfilling. However, he struggled to switch off from work and mentioned that he was divorced and didn't see as much of his two kids as he would like. He described how his company had grown and how he felt he was now losing the 'caring culture' that he had carefully built and nurtured because 'it is just so hard to hold on to with so many people and priorities.'

'What steps have you taken to nurture that culture to date, particularly during this growth period?' I asked.

'Our values are clear, and we make sure we refer to them constantly. We also ask our managers to make regular presentations to talk through the values at their team level. One of our core values is joy and it is important to me that each employee gets joy from their work,' he said.

As Glenn detailed each of the steps he had taken to ensure that their culture was caring for all, I was struck: it was *his* agenda and he had not bothered to engage his people in defining what a caring environment meant *for them*. To address Glenn's challenges, I needed to reach a good cross-section of his people to come to understand how they were receiving Glenn and what they needed from him. To be inclusive, we had to first seek feedback to understand his systemic impact as a leader. Only then would he be able to identify the gaps and understand what 'being included' would look like for his people. I thought about my team and knew that we had our work cut out, but this kind of challenge was our bread-and-butter: kicking off culture change by seeking feedback. I knew that we could, and would, make a difference for Glenn and his people.

We began obtaining and analysing feedback from Glenn's people. When I shared the results with Glenn, he was shocked by how strongly it stressed that his people had felt left out. He had been so keen to keep them joyful that he had put pressure on himself to research what sparked joy in other organisations, but he had forgotten to lean on the true experts on his people – his people themselves.

Why seek feedback?

When prospective clients first get introduced to our SHARE Leadership method, they often ask why we focus on seeking feedback first. Here's why:

Many organisations that we come across focus more heavily on feedback training – often for managers in preparation for performance review conversations – that covers how to give feedback and various feedback giving models and very little (if at all) on how to receive feedback. Even less attention is given to building people's confidence to seek feedback.

Many leaders rely on their organisational processes to gain feedback and they are often unable to confidently articulate how their people feel about their leadership. When we ask about 360-review processes, larger organisations tend to have in-house capabilities to facilitate the process. However, they are either not used effectively or, when they are administered, leaders who receive the feedback reports are not adequately supported to embrace the feedback, effectively bridge their identified development gaps or show their people that they not only welcome the feedback but would like to be held accountable.

When we run our Constructive Conversations workshops, feedback from managers and leaders often points to how ill-equipped they had previously felt to seek feedback, receive feedback and create a culture of accountability between them and their people. This validated my own sense concerning the need for inclusive leaders to prioritise seeking feedback, rather than just giving it. Most professionals have had some training on giving feedback, but not many organisations develop their leaders to effectively seek and receive feedback. It is therefore no surprise that many leaders resist seeking feedback yet still want a strong feedback culture. To shape a feedback culture, leaders should themselves model proactively seeking out, receiving and acting on feedback.

While leaders often understand that feedback is a requirement of good leadership, they are often not clear on what the feedback is for and why they really need it. As a leader, you may have requested feedback as part of a leadership development programme or as part of your organisation's standard processes, but rarely is it because you recognise that you would value and benefit from input from your people.

In my experience of developing leaders over the last decade, I have found that the higher up you rise in your leadership journey, the fewer chances you have of being offered regular, honest and constructive feedback. Given that practice makes perfect, leaders often become increasingly uncomfortable with receiving feedback. Unsurprisingly, you will not find people lining up to offer feedback to you on your leadership, particularly from among your most junior employees. Receiving feedback is too often perceived as likely to be a negative experience, and many professionals that I ask admit to getting defensive when offered feedback, even if that feedback later turns out to be positive or constructive. It will then come as no surprise to you to know that you probably walk around with a distorted sense of who you are as a leader and of your impact on others. Developing your self-awareness is key to learning to embrace and develop from feedback.

Love feedback

Self-awareness is a crucial leadership competency and one that cannot be built effectively without feedback. Every individual has instances where their intentions do not match their impact. My work regularly brings this disparity to light.

In our workshops, I often ask participants when they last offered feedback to their leaders. Unsurprisingly, I often get blank stares. Some of them have never even considered it. When probed further, participants often say that they worry whether their leaders will be open to feedback, and that even if they appear to be receptive, whether they will be able to appreciate and learn from constructive feedback.

How you perceive feedback will influence how much you seek and get offered, but also how well you receive and can embrace and learn from it. Like most leaders, some self-work is necessary before you can see the true value feedback has to offer.

I recently facilitated a conversation with a global leadership team and one of their employee resource groups (ERGs). After a hugely insightful and productive dialogue between the two groups, one of the leaders asked the question, 'Why did it have to take Obi for this discussion to take place?' The truth is, it took a lot of work at previous sessions to build trust and convince the group that this leadership group genuinely wanted to work with them to co-create an inclusive organisation. Creating ERGs and seeking feedback is not enough. You must build trust, learn to welcome all feedback, be open to influence and act on feedback while ensuring that you constantly create safe environments for your people to share.

To truly experience the beauty and value of feedback, you must find ways to stimulate and embrace feedback as a crucial part of your leadership. Making this shift is not an easy journey for leaders, particularly those who fall under the perfectionist archetype.

Leading your brain

Cognitive behavioural therapy (CBT) is a talking therapy that teaches us that, at a basic level, what we think affects how we feel, which in turn affects how we act and then the results we get back.

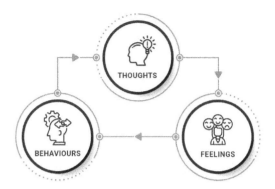

The Thoughts–Feelings–Behaviours Cycle

In my neuroleadership studies, I explored this in more detail. It was a real privilege for me to return to neuroscience, my favourite subject during my physiology degree at University College London. This time, the emphasis was on exploring the neuroscience behind what happens within organisations at times of change, or when solving problems, decision-making and collaborating. I was particularly struck by how, as leaders, we can fuel or limit our performance based on the expectations we place on ourselves. I will share a basic explanation below to develop your understanding of what is happening in your brain when you place unrealistic expectations on yourself. This will help you develop more self-compassion and build your confidence as an inclusive leader.

Let's start with a personal experience that provided an opportunity for me to put my lesson into practice. As part of an organisation-wide delivery of our Shaping

An Inclusive Culture programme, I was to facilitate a workshop for the top leadership team. Although I had already run workshops for the majority of their employees, this was my first meeting with the leadership team and I arrived feeling both excited and slightly nervous.

Reminding myself that I couldn't be more prepared, I kicked off the session with introductions, overall context and then the setup for their first group activity. I had spent hours preparing laminated A4 sheets with some of the feedback from their people which I was going to spread on the floor to allow them to walk around, read and take in. As I asked them to get up, stretch and prepare to walk around, I realised that I had left my folder containing the sheets back in my office!

One of the modules we studied in neuroleadership looked at how we process disappointment in ourselves, and consequently, the impact it has on our actions. When we experience a setback or make a mistake and beat ourselves up over it, the level of dopamine (sometimes referred to as the 'happy hormone') in our brain goes down. This triggers other reactions in our brain and consequently, how we respond. Being mindful, recognising our saboteur-driven thoughts and taking back control of our thinking can make all the difference. Consider this illustration of what could have happened in my brain had I not reminded myself to guide my brain effectively.

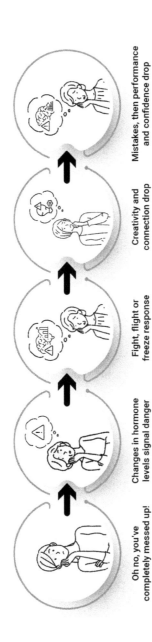

Oh no, you've completely messed up!

Changes in hormone levels signal danger

Fight, flight or freeze response

Creativity and connection drop

Mistakes, then performance and confidence drop

Disappointment in ourselves can lead to changes in the brain that hinder our performance

This can be summarised as follows:

- Thought in my brain: 'Oh no, you've completely messed up!'

- Impact of this thought on my brain: Hormone levels in my brain will be impacted by this self-critical way I think about this experience. One of those hormones, dopamine (the 'happy hormone') will drop, alerting my brain that something is wrong.

- This will result in production of the stress hormone, triggering a fight/flight/freeze response.

- This response shuts down the calming parasympathetic nervous system needed to identify creative solutions to potentially stressful or dangerous situations. I end up making poor decisions and possibly more mistakes.

- My performance and consequently confidence will drop.

My initial thought when I discovered the forgotten sheets was that I could 'wing it' and find a way to muddle through without admitting that I had made a mistake. Instead, I was able to use my understanding of the potentially negative impact on my brain and thought processes to guide my decision to confess my mistake to the participants and ask for a moment to think. Because I had controlled the potential processes within my brain, I was able come up with a reasonable alternative plan and I asked the participants to take a short break while I got my HR contact in the organisation to help me make fresh copies. I had also been able to seize this as an opportunity to demonstrate the value of vulnerability and self-compassion, reinforcing the idea that we are all human and normalising making mistakes.

In my work developing leaders to reframe feedback, I am always struck by how frequently leaders go through the same ineffective ways of perceiving feedback, and in doing so, trigger the limiting cycle described above, which benefits no one. Imagine what would be different at work – and beyond – if everyone learned to consider feedback as an opportunity to identify and address the gap between intention and impact rather than as a criticism.

Your impact, not your intention

When you find yourself judging someone or complaining about somebody, take a moment to consider that their impact on you might not match their intention. Oftentimes, our saboteurs lead us to judge people through their impact without considering that their intentions might differ. If you are reading this book, you will probably be able to identify certain situations or relationships where you are unsure of how others are perceiving you. You can probably see that to address this you should be asking for feedback, yet you hold back, afraid of what you could receive.

This disparity between intention and impact often comes to light when I share the impact that leaders have on me during our interactions. Similarly, when I debrief clients' 360-degree feedback reports, they are often surprised by the results. Like most coaches, as part of our screening process before we take on a new client, we offer them a complimentary session to check that they are right for us and vice versa. If I find that a prospective client's values are not aligned to ours, I will tell them that I am unable to work with them and will recommend a more suitable service provider. This usually come as a surprise, and for some, it can be the first time they have had a service provider say no to their business.

Take my experience with Peter, who came across as offputtingly arrogant in our first meeting, where he spoke repeatedly about how powerful he was. He seemed to know how to handle every situation, and he knew how others should too! Hearing him talk, I felt anxious and recognised that I was not excited about the prospect of working with him. I kept pondering why he had reached out for coaching. Was it just to get someone else to stroke his ego? I decided to share my thoughts and anxieties with him. I told him that I did not see how I could help as he seemed to have all things, past, present and future, sorted.

To my surprise, he started welling up and then crying! He explained that over the years he had built up a protective facade of being in control and that he had also lost connection to others. By giving himself permission to lose the facade, he could finally begin to explore the voice of his saboteur, the weight of the facade he had created and ultimately, his need to change. It was then that we really connected, and I was able to see how our coaching could help him learn to grow and trust his authentic and truly powerful self.

Receiving regular feedback is an opportunity for you to explore how you are impacting others, and to ensure that this is aligned with your intentions. There will always be times and situations where they are not. Effective self-leadership requires that you continuously check in with your people to get a sense of your impact on others, and where necessary, ensure that any mismatch is tackled effectively.

So, what gets in the way?

Fear of feedback

Fear stops leaders inviting regular feedback and other perspectives on their performance. Fear also gets in the way of leaders receiving feedback effectively. I often come across leaders who have never sought honest feedback before my request that they do so.

However, just inviting feedback is not enough. Fear can also impact on your people's ability to give feedback. You must ensure that the feedback space that you create feels sufficiently comfortable and safe for your people to open up to providing truly honest and constructive feedback.

When we facilitate focus group sessions to discuss themes from anonymous feedback results from in-house employee opinion surveys, we often discover that participants have heavily censored their views. I asked one team member why she had felt the need to sugar-coat her responses to an employee opinion survey: 'We all know that you can't trust that they are truly anonymised. I have to protect myself as my feedback could impact my relationship with my boss.' She described fearing that honest feedback could damage that relationship, particularly if her boss felt that it had partly contributed to unwanted outcomes such as a promotion stalling or a reduction in his bonus.

Recognising that there is a widespread fear of feedback, but also accepting that you cannot be an inclusive leader without receiving ongoing feedback from your people, you will have to set about proactively exploring and breaking down some of the fears and myths surrounding feedback and how it is processed within your organisation. Two key methods to achieve this are to make seeking direct feedback a regular feature of your leadership and by frequently modelling how honest and constructive feedback can be truly and generously embraced.

Reframe feedback

Before you can get yourself ready to make seeking feedback a habit, you must learn to receive feedback effectively, trusting in your ability to embrace and accept it willingly. Your saboteur will tell you that feedback is a criticism and an attack. That is hardly surprising, given the traditional view of feedback. Most leaders will confess that the word 'feedback' frightens them, bringing with it the suggestion of accusations or punishment. Even just the idea of being offered feedback often raises anxiety levels, increasing their resistance to seeking feedback. We have already explored the negative thought and behavioural cycle that will then result.

Let us explore an alternative perspective. Feedback provides a range of opportunities, including the chance to investigate how you are being received by others and identify any gaps between impact and intention, to celebrate where you have made a positive impact and to recognise where you need to make changes as you continue on our development journey. Before you can reframe feedback for others, you must ensure that you have genuinely embraced the opportunities it presents yourself. This is a good time to revisit and review your work on the saboteur voice and mindset shifts.

One of the best examples of reframing feedback that I have come across was from a senior leader in a multinational company who explained that he asks his people for 'advice', not 'feedback'. This reframing presents a powerful incentive, both for the giver and the receiver. Most people enjoy helping others. Neuroscience can explain why: as social beings, helping others causes the release of 'happy hormones' (such as serotonin, dopamine and oxytocin) in our brains, which in turn boost our moods and bring us joy. We may well feel pride that our opinions are being sought and pleased that they are evidently valued, and in return, we give generously. How wonderful it is then that asking others for advice can increase all-round positivity!

Another way to open people's minds to both the giving and receiving of feedback is to make sure that you model giving feedback with the right balance between what many would consider positive feedback, or praise, versus negative feedback or criticism. Researchers Emily Heaphy and consultant Marcial Losada studied the role of positivity and connectivity in the performance of business teams and established that the ideal ratio is five positive comments to one negative interaction or criticism.[26]

I have facilitated hundreds of feedback sessions over the last decade, and I have yet to come across one person who could not see value in received feedback when given the opportunity to reframe and embrace it. With Peter, I had to be fiercely outspoken in telling him I found he came across as arrogant before he could then pause and truly hear what his colleagues were trying to ask of him. When he took the opportunity to reflect on his unintended impact, he was then able to identify numerous instances where his intentions had not been clear to his team members.

If received openly and fully embraced, every piece of feedback you receive contains some nugget of information that can help you to grow. We may find initially that we want to reject the perceived threat posed by negative feedback, but reframe the intent behind feedback for you and your people and you have made a key step to providing yourself with growth opportunities to listen and learn from those around you.

Biases

In Part One of this book, you started learning more about yourself, what drives you and how you show up as a leader. As you begin to open up to seeking feedback from your people, you may also notice that you tend to navigate towards people that are more like you.

Neuroscience teaches us that our brain is always scanning the environment to identify differences and change, both of which could ultimately pose a threat. It is this ability that has helped us survive and evolve as humans, but it does mean that we are inherently biased. As a leader, you cannot be truly inclusive unless you take time to expose, identify and confront your biases.

Each of us holds countless biases that have developed based on our personal life experiences, background, environments and influences. Socialisation is the process through which individuals learn to build beliefs about the world around them based on what they are exposed to. With that in mind, letting go requires that you make a conscious decision to get curious about the subconscious judgements that you make, what informs them and how they have guided you as a leader. Question yourself on your biases, asking yourself which you hold dear and which you might choose to challenge. Learn to step into others' shoes and build empathy so that these unintentional judgements do not dictate your leadership, inadvertently driving you to exclude people who are less like you.

Challenging these biases is another area where seeking feedback is invaluable. By understanding where your biases come from and regularly checking in on how you are being perceived by your diverse people, you will get to know yourself better and can self-correct where needed. This will help you ensure that you are inclusive as you engage your people in developing you as the leader they can trust. Go a step further and extend this commitment to processes and systems that you influence as a leader – identify areas where your teams or organisation could be excluding others, let go of coming up with solutions and engage diverse people in coming up with inclusive ways forward.

Cohesion is good, but it can be negative when it excludes and marginalises differences. It feeds groupthink which often occurs at the expense of inclusion of diversity and sharing leadership.

 NUGGETS FOR REFLECTION AND ACTION

Reflect on and journal your responses to the following:

- As an inclusive leader, how could you reconnect with your people, step back and make space for their diversity to influence the direction of your services, products or organisation?
- Which team members do you not know well, and how does that get in the way of you advocating for them?
- At work and beyond, which communities of nondominant groups could you get to know better? Which resources could help you build a better awareness of people less like you?
- Which biases might get in the way of you being an inclusive leader?
- What is unspoken about who is welcome and made to feel at home in your team or organisation?

- Consider areas where you may inadvertently be feeding groupthink, excluding or marginalising diversity under the guise of cohesion. Where do you need to challenge yourself and your teams on this?

Just do it

By now, you recognise that you cannot be inclusive without understanding that your impact will not always match your intention. To counter this, you must practise and prioritise regularly seeking feedback and ensuring that it becomes part of your culture. One way to do this is to start right away. Build seeking feedback into your working culture: perhaps check in with people at the start and end of your day or week? Learn to ask for feedback in regular interactions such as your team meetings: 'How would you rate today's team meeting on a scale of one to ten? If not yet ten, what would make it a ten?'

Regularly seeking and inviting feedback will reduce fear and encourage the giving of it, empowering your people to advise on what is working in your leadership. Doing so regularly will also provide an opportunity to normalise discussing and acknowledging mistakes and weakness, demonstrating to your people that it is healthy and strong to be vulnerable enough to ask for their help in identifying and exploring areas where you may have got things wrong or need to improve, while also demonstrating to them that their opinions and input matter.

 NUGGETS FOR REFLECTION AND ACTION

Reflect on and journal your responses to the following:

- To what extent do your people know that their opinions on your leadership matter?
- When did you last actively seek out their opinions and suggestions for your leadership development?
- When did you last undertake a 360-degree feedback process with your team?
- Where could you use feedback from your people on how you are leading?
- Can you make a commitment to ask your people for advice on any areas where you could use fresh perspectives?
- How could you build in seeking feedback as a regular feature of your leadership?

 **Key lessons**

In this chapter, you have read about the value of seeking and receiving feedback as a way to get to know yourself better. You have further developed your self-awareness and learned that:

- The more senior you become, the more seeking feedback must be a key part of your approach to leadership.

- Your mindset on feedback and what it means will influence how you seek and receive feedback.

- Your mindset on feedback directly influences your brain and the hormones that determine whether or not you can effectively learn from the feedback you receive and use it to fuel better leadership behaviours.

- Feedback is an invaluable opportunity for you to constantly gauge how closely your intentions match your impact.

- To create a feedback culture, you as a leader must model the right behaviours of not just effectively giving feedback, but seeking, receiving and acting on feedback.

- Through regular feedback you will uncover unconscious biases that can derail your efforts to be an inclusive leader if not acknowledged and addressed.

6
H – Have Accountability

If you have effective accountability in your team, you are united by a shared purpose, with clear roles and responsibilities within it. There is transparency in the way individual and team performance is assessed through measures such as key performance indicators (KPI) and an understanding of how everyone contributes to your collective success.

As a leader, you work for your people as much as they work for you. One of the most surprising lessons that I learned when I first began my journey in developing leaders is that many leaders do not feel accountable to their people, instead assuming that it is the job of a leader to hold others accountable, but not vice versa. Challenging this assumption has become a key part of our work in developing inclusive leaders and we are always keen to instil in teams an understanding of this mutual accountability as soon as the leader and team members feel sufficiently empowered for us to do so.

You cannot be an inclusive leader unless you establish yourself as being answerable to the ways you lead and the decisions you make as a leader. Consider Mikko, who had invited me and my colleague to coach his global team. Their initial team diagnostic performance report already revealed that this team rated itself poorly on decision-making. They felt that prior decisions were all too frequently changed, resulting in reduced engagement in new processes and a reluctance to commit. As one team member described: 'New processes are likely to get pulled before they stick, so there is no point wasting too much time and energy on getting to grips with them.'

At the coaching session, my colleague and I walked the participants through an exercise that was designed to help teams explore what holds them back. A few steps into the activity, Mikko was hit by an 'aha' moment: 'I have just realised that when I make commitments to this team, particularly on how I will support new processes, I sometimes don't follow through and no one has challenged me on that before. As a matter of fact, accountability is something we have all struggled with in this team.'

The look on the faces around the room was priceless! One of the team members started to speak up to reassure him, but Mikko interrupted: 'It's OK. As a leader, I have always talked about accountability. I have seen my job as holding you all accountable, but I should have asked all of you to do the same for me. It's my job to ask for your support. I'm sorry, I could have saved us all a lot of time if I had facilitated team accountability from the start. Let's start changing that now.'

This was the perfect opportunity for us to start coaching the team on how best to hold their leader, and one another, accountable. In this chapter, you will explore the topics that came up when coaching Mikko and his team. You will pick up lessons from the actions that he took to get his team more engaged and to start holding one another accountable.

Leadership responsibility

It takes courage to be an accountable leader. New leaders often become so excited by their roles that they fail to recognise that leadership is not just an opportunity, but also a huge responsibility, with expectations from all angles. The decision-makers that agreed to offer you your leadership role place their confidence in you. That vote carries a risk that their judgement may be called into question if you mess up or fail.

The people that you lead will also look to you with expectations. You are likely to find that some have experienced poor leadership in the past and now view you with suspicion because they are so used to being let down. Others may be grieving the loss of the previous leader and may even begin to idolise your predecessor. In the process, they might place additional expectations on you to lead in a particular way and to an unrealistically elevated standard.

Having a clear sense of who you are, your leadership vision, your strengths and your development needs as an inclusive leader will ensure you are fully prepared to introduce yourself to your people, share your aspirations, explore how best you can lead them and ask for accountability. That responsibility is not one to be taken lightly, but you can make the decision to embrace it and include your people at any and every stage of your leadership journey.

Culture of accountability

You cannot build a feedback culture without account-ability being part of that culture. An inclusive leader ensures that they are held accountable as leaders, team members and as individuals. They shape teams that understand, embrace and prioritise their collec-tive responsibility for sustaining an inclusive culture. Accountability must live across the organisation and there must be systems in place for checking in on that culture. Without accountability, productivity drops, followed by engagement and morale.

How can you as a leader shape a culture of account-ability? A couple of years ago, my colleague and I facilitated a two-day offsite coaching session for a 100-person department of a large engineering com-pany. They had recently received the report from their employee opinion survey and the leadership team were surprised by the low scores for being 'one team'. It seemed that the teams within the department tended to work in isolation from one another, even when the efficiency of one team directly impacted the efficiency of others. We needed to break down these restrictive silos, but to do this, we needed first to build their awareness of their respective strengths, chal-lenges and frustrations. Only then could they look at how best to support one another, collaborate and co-create. Most importantly, they needed to ensure accountability across the board.

131

Rather than focus on coaching the leadership team to solve the identified challenges, we encouraged them to let go of being the problem solvers. First, we needed them to share leadership and to experience the department working as one team.

We designed an exercise to help the entire department gain a deeper understanding of one another's business landscapes and to explore how they could boost others by fostering synergy between teams. As part of the exercise, we invited each team to try occupying another team's table and attempting to tackle their key challenges. They all made impressive recommendations for their colleagues and each team returned to find their home table now brimming with ideas. We then moved on to the Empower stage of our SHARE Leadership method (covered later in this book), and as we began wrapping up, the leaders were surprised to hear how motivated each team now felt to take on more collaborative opportunities, gain better exposure and start being held accountable by others. Participants shared that they had previously struggled to empathise with others outside their own teams because they had little understanding of others' experiences, so had unrealistic expectations of them.

For the first time, the leadership team recognised that they had huge untapped creativity, innovation and drive in their organisation. All they had needed to start shaping a culture of accountability was to let go of coming up with the answers themselves, bring everyone together, build stronger connections and, ultimately, share leadership.

 NUGGETS FOR REFLECTION AND ACTION

Reflect on and journal your responses to the following:

- What would a culture of accountability look like in your relationship with your people?

- To what extent do you marginalise creativity by not inviting your people to co-create solutions and take responsibility for accountability – with you, for you and for one another?

Abuse of power

Leadership always comes with influence, responsibility and power. Your position as a leader demands that people look up to you, bringing with it a responsibility to guide and influence their development, productivity, engagement, career progression and wellbeing. The power bestowed on you by leadership can be dangerous if you do not take the time to understand it fully, occupy the role effectively and make a firm commitment to use this power in service of those that do not have it. As with any power, it can be abused, and leaders may unintentionally abuse their power if they feel threatened. In coaching sessions, it is often only when we relay feedback to the client on their impact, using either the 360-degree feedback from their people or the coach's own experience of working with the client, that this realisation becomes clear.

Both as an in-house HR professional and in my later coaching work, I frequently supported professionals in transitioning out of toxic workplace relationships and roles, and I heard many first-hand stories from those impacted by abuse of power. Sometimes it occurred because the leaders in question did not invite constructive feedback so had little or no awareness of their impact on others; other times it was because the organisations they served did not call out unacceptable behaviour so abuse of power was permitted not just to live within their organisations, but to thrive. Newer leaders to the organisation would emulate these same poor leadership behaviours, while simultaneously lamenting the incessant absenteeism, burnout and attrition levels.

To ensure that you do not abuse your leadership power, you need to bring your people closer. Ensure that you are clear on your shared purpose. What is your team or organisation's shared purpose, and is every member clear on this and on how their role feeds into it? What do your people need from you as their leader to ensure they are set up for success in their roles? Ask them how best you can use your influence to enable them to bring their full selves to work, feel a sense of belonging and feel empowered to walk beside you instead of behind. Most importantly, ask them how they could hold you accountable for being and staying inclusive.

Clear expectations

You cannot have a culture of accountability without clear expectations. In our team coaching workshops, confusion around expectations is often at the root of many disagreements and strained relationships. Often the leader is unclear on their own expectations and thus communications around these are unclear, ill-considered or poorly formed. Too often, expectations are assumed rather than clearly laid out, leading to the waste of already limited resources on tasks that are not a priority for the team or the business.

As an inclusive leader, you are responsible for clarifying and communicating your expectations to your team, but you must also be clear on your team's expectations of you. When did you last check in with your teams on how you are doing and, perhaps more importantly, on how that matches their expectations of you as their leader?

Here is an extract from a conversation with an executive coaching client, Mo:

Me: Are your teams happy with the way you lead them?

Mo: [Long pause] I guess so.

Me: How come you're not sure?

Mo: Well, I couldn't really be, could I?

Me: Why not?

Mo: [Thinking silently for some time before answering] I guess I could ask. I really should ask.

 NUGGETS FOR REFLECTION AND ACTION

Reflect on and journal your responses to the following:

- When did you last clarify your expectations of your team with them? Did you explore how closely you, and they, feel they are meeting those expectations?
- When did you last clarify your team's expectations of you? Did you explore how closely they, and you, feel you are meeting those expectations?

Turf wars

If, as a leader, you do not provide clear expectations and direction, roles and responsibilities can become muddled and turf wars may start to emerge as people move to protect their territories. Conflict often arises from duplicated efforts due to confusion and uncertainty over respective responsibility and accountability. This risks key priorities falling through the gaps and can ultimately lead to poor decision-making and weak performance.

Consider this example. I was invited by an organisation to mediate between two senior colleagues that found themselves at loggerheads. Both led teams that were crucial to the success of a critical cross-functional initiative launched after the organisation lost a major bid. This significant loss was now fuelling concerns about the business projections and fears of job losses throughout the organisation. Their boss, Jide, was becoming frustrated as the conflict between the two teams meant that they were withholding key information from each other and the competition was increasingly unhealthy.

I invited Jide to join the initial stages of my contracting meeting with the two colleagues. Within minutes it became clear that the conflict stemmed from a lack of clarity on expectations, augmented by a lack of transparency from Jide about the general direction of the business. Both colleagues were desperate to prove themselves as each had become convinced that amid the current uncertainty the business could not afford to retain them both at the same level. This was far more than just a turf war! The two feared that they were in direct competition for just one position; each was desperate to prove their capability over the other. Jide was shocked. Although the loss of the bid had been painful, both personally and for the business, the situation was nowhere near as bleak as the warring colleagues had understood. Jide just needed to be transparent about the situation and share information with the colleagues about other opportunities that he was exploring! Ultimately, although ostensibly personal, the conflict was in reality a reaction to systemic fear, insecurity and a lack of direction.

 NUGGETS FOR REFLECTION AND ACTION

Reflect on and journal your responses to the following:

- As an inclusive leader, where in your leadership might you need to provide more transparency and clarity?

Transparency

Most people who know me, either from work or outside, know that I am a huge advocate for transparency. I firmly believe that transparency can heal, and better still, prevent most relationship challenges. Too often it is fear of conflict that holds people back from sharing key information, necessary feedback or demands and requests with those around them. The result of this reticence is that connection and cohesion suffer, and trust can be damaged.

Our brains crave certainty. If we do not know something, we make it up. This is one of the reasons that rumours flourish in organisations. Furthermore, because evolution has shaped our brain to remain constantly alert for threats, in this uncertainty we're likely to imagine the worst-case scenario. As an inclusive leader, you are accountable to your people for always providing as much certainty as possible. When you hold back, you leave space for misinformation, misinterpretation and fear, and trust can start to dwindle.

Even your silence can be mined for meaning by those left in the dark. Your saboteur may encourage you to remain quiet for fear of saying the wrong things or convince you that it is better to wait until you have more information to share. In contrast, my experience of developing inclusive organisations has shown me, time and again, that you can never communicate too much. One of your most important responsibilities as a leader is to be open with your people and to share as much as you can at any given time.

Of course, there will be times when full disclosure to everyone is not appropriate. This could be when matters concern specific individuals, potential organisational changes, or compliance and regulatory information that could cause unnecessary anxieties or leave your organisation vulnerable if shared prematurely.

In those circumstances, you may feel tempted to stay silent, hiding away from any communication or conversations with others until you are ready. However, this lack of transparency opens up that damaging space where uncertainty and misinformation grow and may give rise to gossip and rumours which can be damaging to individuals, your culture and ultimately, your business. It is far better to be upfront and simply acknowledge that you do have confidential information that you are not currently able to share. Leaders often forget that their people will understand and accept that this privilege comes with leadership, but they will appreciate your acknowledgement of this. Your transparency in such situations will be reassuring for your people, building their trust in you and enabling you to support them as they navigate any feelings of uncertainty.

I once saw this transparency so beautifully modelled by a leader in a team coaching session as she announced to her team her decision to step down:

> 'I wish I could say much more at this stage, but I can't. However, it should come as no surprise that two of you in this team would be in line to take over from me. I will fully support you two throughout the selection process and I would like to invite this team to do the same. There is no question that either one of you would make a success of this role, and whatever decision is reached, your capability would not be a question. I just wish we had two roles.'

What a brilliant way to be transparent to her team while also inviting them to join her in supporting their colleagues!

NUGGETS FOR REFLECTION AND ACTION

Reflect on and journal your responses to the following:

- Think about how open and transparent you are with your people. Are there times and places where you could have shared more than you did? What made you hold back?
- What might your people say to the above questions if you asked them?
- Where could you share more with your people and what process will you put in place as a reminder to keep checking in on how transparent you are as a leader?

Coaching

For me, coaching has been life-changing, and I was already a huge advocate long before I made the decision to transition into becoming a full-time executive coach.

In my final in-house role, I worked as a trainer, mentor, learning and development consultant, and coach to various leaders. However, it was not until I completed my coach qualification that I really appreciated how my coach training now enabled me to offer people something completely different. Through my newfound and consistent approach to development, clients developed their self-awareness and independence. By placing the expertise firmly in their hands, I allowed them to build greater confidence and the ability not only to tackle their immediate challenges, but to identify and nurture possibilities.

The Adapt phase of our SHARE Leadership method is designed to develop you to guide your people to make changes and then sustain them independently. It is about learning to identify your own weaknesses and blind spots, letting go while staying fully supportive, and constructively challenging others to grow while ensuring that you do not get in the way of their progression. It is also about accepting, acknowledging and constantly assessing accountability, to yourself and to your people.

Measures

I love measures and assessment scales! It is fascinating to me how little we value and use the process of measuring our achievements as leaders. If you prioritise accountability, finding ways to quantify progress and recognise success should not be a challenge.

However, you cannot measure how far you have come without marking a starting point. I often ask my executive coaching clients to describe how inclusive they are as leaders at any given time. Many struggle initially to respond confidently to that question, often because they have not been intentional about their commitment to being inclusive. Many have never paused to identify a clear starting point in their journey, alongside their people, to becoming inclusive.

So, what could be a starting point to measuring how inclusive you are as a leader? Consider what might happen if you asked your team a question: 'What are three ways in which leaders can become more inclusive?' Let's assume that they respond with the following suggestions:

1. Engage the team in setting team expectations

2. Regularly seek feedback on their leadership impact

3. Know their people well enough to understand what it would take for them to feel a strong sense of belonging within your organisation

You then ask them to rate your current performance on the first of these suggestions: 'On a scale of 1–10, to what extent do I engage you in setting team expectations?' Their answer to this will become your starting point. You then follow this with a second question: 'What would a ten on this scale look like?' This represents their expectation of you. Their answers on each of the suggestions will identify how and why you should regularly seek feedback, measure progress and share leadership as an inclusive leader.

This process of identifying the destination, marking the starting point and outlining the journey is a method of measurement that can be applied to countless areas of your leadership, and your team's and business's performance. Using a numerical scale also makes it possible for you to provide quantitative results following reassessment, such as by enabling you to identify that you have had an X% increase in a particular area of development.

Key lessons

Inclusive leaders engage their people in creating expectations of them as leaders and of one another. To create an accountable culture, your people need clarity on:

- How you use your power as a leader, and where they can hold you accountable

- Your collective purpose and direction

- Their individual roles and responsibilities, and how they support one another

- What is going on at any given time, even if that involves sharing that you have nothing you can share

- How they, and you, can measure their success in keeping you accountable

7
A – Adapt

As an inclusive leader, you must continually adapt and evolve. In previous chapters, you have explored various ways in which you should question, challenge and modify your perception and performance as a leader to become inclusive.

In this chapter, you will consider how you can prepare and support your people so that they too can undertake the same shifts in perception and expectation of the leadership experience, as you let go and share more. You will learn how to create an environment that invites and welcomes your people to share the wisdom, creativity and ideas that their diverse experiences, perspectives and approaches can offer to your organisation.

Consider this debrief session with Simone after I held a coaching session for her team. She had become visibly frustrated during the team session and I wanted to learn more about what had been going on for her:

Me: I could sense that you were frustrated today and that then had an impact on your team. Do you know why you felt this way?

Simone: I felt angry and misunderstood.

Me: Can I share my observations?

Simone: Yes, please. I don't know what it is that I'm not seeing.

Me: Your desire to problem-solve is a huge strength, but it can also be your blind spot.

In today's session, your team confided in you that they were feeling insecure about the future. Your response was to jump in to rescue them. You went on to give them a speech about resilience and confidence.

Simone: How is that wrong?

Me: It wasn't, but it just wasn't what they needed at that time. My sense is that all they wanted was a space for them to share their feelings and for you to listen and understand.

Simone: That would explain why they suddenly seemed to shut down, just nodding and giving me nothing back, which in turn made me increasingly frustrated.

Me: There was an opportunity there for you to encourage them to share more about how they were feeling and to invite them to explore together what lay behind those feelings and to problem-solve with you. Perhaps you could have asked how they felt you could best support them, or you could have invited them to explore with you how best you could all be in this uncertainty together.

The coaching session between Simone and her team had offered several missed opportunities for exchanges like this. Simone and I spent some time reviewing the experience and exploring how, next time, she could let go of rescuing and adapt her approach to better recognise and then use these opportunities to start sharing leadership more. She walked away from our coaching session with tools to support her on her own inclusive leadership development journey, but this change did not impact only Simone.

When I met with the team again a few months later to review a recent product launch, I barely recognised them. They were more connected and cohesive as one team and there was a buzz in the room as they shared experiences, came up with new ideas and celebrated one another! Had Simone continued with her previous leadership approach, I doubt that she could have survived that period without burnout. Not only would the product launch have been disastrous, but she was at significant risk of losing key talent from her team, further increasing her frustrations and stress. Simone had acknowledged the need to change and adapted, and in doing so, she had also transformed her team.

In this chapter, I will share the lessons and tools that developed Simone's ability to adapt and create an inclusive culture where leadership was shared.

Influences and assumptions

Over the course of this book so far, you have identified some of the influences that have contributed to you becoming the leader that you are today. To share leadership and become inclusive, it is equally important to examine the different factors that may have influenced the diverse people that you work with and how they now present at work. With that knowledge, you will be able to consider where you may need to let go, adapt or modify how you lead to ensure that you can shape an inclusive workplace that motivates each of them to be and do their best. Without undertaking this process of examination and adaptation, you will make poor judgements and risk inadvertently growing stronger connections with those who are more like you and in the process marginalising those that are not.

I will share my own experiences. Born in Germany, growing up in Nigeria and Finland and now living in London, UK, I have been exposed to a particularly wide range of different cultures, people and experiences. I have been influenced to some degree by each of these and I am able to draw from this enviable richness in my various leadership roles.

Let us consider how these influences play out in practice. I was facilitating a mediation meeting between a client service team and one of their key stakeholders who had submitted a complaint about being disrespected by the team. When I met Yemi, the Nigerian businesswoman that had complained, she was totally unlike the person the all-white client service team had described to me. She was incredibly passionate about their partnership and spoke proudly about her vision for the work they were doing, but she was feeling demotivated. She explained that a couple of the team members had been disrespectful to her, and I could see the impact they had on her. When I brought them all together, I saw how some of the team were misla-belling Yemi's genuine passion for the project as her being 'argumentative'. Allowing space for Yemi to speak and be heard led to a much deeper understand-ing, with the team recognising that they had indeed been disrespectful and had shut her out of decisions when she should have been involved.

I can relate strongly to Yemi's experience. My daugh-ters often tease me that when I have some of my Nigerian buddies over or on the phone, we do noth-ing but argue! For us, these times are when we are having our most exciting and passionate conversa-tions! I could share many more examples of cultural differences that I have experienced between my mostly confident American friends, my predomi-nantly reserved Finnish relatives, or from leadership coaching clients that have been raised by leaders to believe that it is their job to call all the shots.

While the first step is recognising that we are each a product of all our influences and upbringing, the big-gest part of the adaptation that you must make as an inclusive leader is to accept and embrace not know-ing, so that you can let go and share. Do not make assumptions about why your people show up the way they do, their influences, what they need or how best to lead them. You cannot know unless you ask.

Assumptions feed stereotyping and will ultimately limit inclusion.

Vulnerability

For centuries, there has been a widely held belief that leaders must demonstrate strength, have all the answers and lead from the front. Embracing 'not knowing' and asking for help is therefore particularly challenging for many leaders, an observation that explains the magnitude of stress, burnout and resignation that I so often find among my executive coaching clients at the start of their coaching journeys. These are symptoms that I recognised from my days in HR in investment banking. Executive and managing directors were often placed on a pedestal and subjected to unrealistic expectations and hugely damaging levels of stress and pressure that led many to burn out before they could ask for help.

When I left the corporate world, I vowed never to work in the sector again. My coach training had unlocked in me a heartfelt desire to be more authentic and I told myself that this unhealthy insistence on appearing to 'have it all together' all of the time was exclusively a banking sector phenomenon. I still remember a conversation with the manager at my first annual review with a new public sector organisation.

'You are too "investment banking",' she said.

'What do you mean by that?' I asked defensively.

'You have incredibly high expectations of yourself, and you expect the same of others.'

'And that's bad because…?' I asked, truthfully not understanding how this could possibly be a problem.

With hindsight, this conversation was an invitation to bring more vulnerability to my leadership. Financial services had taught me that self-confidence was a necessity and that being powerful was to be desired and celebrated; prudence, self-doubt or any expression of vulnerability were understood as unacceptable signs of weakness and therefore to be quashed or hidden for fear of criticism. This culture was truly embedded within me, as my new manager had identified, and it was only when I first learned to embrace and celebrate my own vulnerability that I was able to truly connect with others and to give them permission to bring their full selves to work.

Inclusive leaders bring their full selves to work and in doing so, acknowledge that they do not have all the answers. They embrace the power that comes through vulnerability, asking for help and working with others to shape a culture where people have permission to make mistakes and to lean into one another. Better solutions are co-created, deeper connections are built and trusting relationships mean that there is a shared belief that together, much more can be achieved.

Ask for help

You cannot be an inclusive leader without including others on your own journey. The starting point of the change you are making must be humility, letting go, choosing to say that you do not have the answers and to ask for help. Draw others in beside you by empowering them with your own vulnerability. Get used to admitting that, 'I don't know,' and to asking others, 'What's the best way to learn more?'

After the horrendous murder of George Floyd, I posted a video on LinkedIn in which I talked about the impact on me as a mother to two black children.[27] Soon after, I received an email from a colleague, Anne, whom I knew only a little through our shared work as board members:

Dear Obi,

I am thinking of you and reflecting on some of what you so generously shared in your video. I don't know what to do, but for a start I just wanted to say I don't have any words to express what I feel, have been feeling all these horrible weeks. I can't start to imagine what it is to feel this for a lifetime… or for one's children.

I wanted to pick up the phone but don't have your number. I hope that if my words are perhaps clumsy and wrong, you will know my note comes from the heart.

If you can tell me what I can do, to not just listen and stand, but to act, please tell me.

With a hug, your friend

I welled up as I read the email, because I could imagine how tough it had been for her to write. My colleague's willingness to make herself so vulnerable before me, acknowledging that she might make mistakes but asking for my forgiveness and assistance to learn, was incredibly powerful, and she is now someone that I proudly call friend.

Many leaders I come across have put themselves under unsustainable pressure by maintaining the expectation that it is always their responsibility alone to know all the answers to all the problems, or to find them if they do not. This is incredibly unhealthy and restrictive as it limits opportunities for them to engage their people, grow their inclusive leadership skills and adapt to meet the development needs of their people.

Team meetings

Every team needs a diversity of voices and influences, but just introducing diversity in membership will not alone result in an equity of influence. I can usually identify the power imbalance in teams just by observing a team's regular meeting. Usually run by the team leader, they may even get cancelled or rescheduled when the team leader is unable to join.

As a leader, you need to ensure that you regularly leave space for people to speak to you and with you, and to co-own your dedicated time with them. A good forum for that space would be your team meetings. To allow space for curiosity, sharing and connection, ensure that meeting agendas are not always driven by you as a leader. Learn to let go and step back, leaving time to develop your team members' confidence to participate, constructively challenge and lead one another. Consider varying who runs each meeting or try breaking up the meeting to let different team members lead different parts of the agenda.

When I lead project teams, we share the responsibility for running the meetings and rotate the roles of facilitator, timekeeper and minute-taker between all members. Each of these roles provides invaluable opportunities for team members to build confidence and key leadership skills:

- As facilitator, they take charge and run the meetings, collating agenda items from others in advance.

- As timekeeper, they work with team members to allocate times to each agenda item and it is their job to move the meetings along to ensure all items are covered. They learn to stay focused and practise holding other team members accountable.

- As minute-taker, they track key action points and ensure they are effectively captured during the meeting and dispersed to everyone afterwards.

When a team leader first trials this idea of rotating roles and responsibilities, many comment that, although relieved of the expectation on them alone to drive the meetings, they feel strange 'just keeping time' or taking the notes. If they can sit with this initial discomfort, over time the leaders cannot help but be amazed at how much more engaging and inclusive their team meetings have become. This is a great and easy first step to letting go and sharing leadership with your team. Will you try it?

Voting

As you let go and become more inclusive, you will become increasingly aware that you may have created a culture that has your people always looking to you for solutions. You will learn that when it comes to decision-making, your vote can influence their votes. They may have become dependent on you and your leadership.

Prior to undertaking coach training, I was seen as a solid problem solver. Challenging and adapting this was something I really struggled with as I transitioned from expert to coach and learned to start trusting that people are often the true experts on what is best for them. In most cases, your people don't need you as a leader to solve their problems and provide solutions. Instead, inclusive leadership requires that you develop your people to build confidence in their own judgements, explore different perspectives and think through options before making the decisions that are best for them. For me, just understanding this was not enough. I often still catch myself sneaking in my votes and telling others what I think is best for them. Inclusive leadership requires a commitment to ongoing personal development, accountability and feedback.

As a leader, you will probably face similar challenges, particularly given that, like me, it was probably your impressive problem-solving abilities that got you to the senior position you are in today. As inclusive leaders who plan to survive and thrive in today's VUCA world, we must unlearn and relearn this skill, recognising that what got us this far won't get us to the next level.

So how do you change? The first step is to recognise just how often you drive others' decisions and then make a conscious decision to stop. Consider all the ways you may convey expectations and lead people to decisions that you believe would be right for them. Be aware that we exert influence in many ways, not just through verbal communication. Your facial expressions, nods, sounds and body language all convey a lot about how you feel and what you are thinking. Learn to catch yourself too and consciously choose to let go and give space for others to problem-solve.

In a team coaching session, a senior leader was listening to his team presenting their ideas for an initiative that was about to be rolled out. Even though he was saying all the right things, it became clear that his team did not believe he really cared. Before the team leader left, he requested that I speak to his team and gather feedback to share with him. They described how the strong negative impact of his body language – checking his watch, looking out the window and even interrupting someone with an unrelated question – had totally undermined any conviction in his words. Remember that being totally present in your interactions with your people is you demonstrating that they matter and that you care. Pay attention and ensure that your body, words and behaviour all convey this consistent message – and mean it, of course!

Zip it

Knowing when to be silent is one of your most powerful tools as an inclusive leader. Learn to ask a question or make a comment, but then zip it! This is a common mistake among those actively undertaking the journey towards becoming inclusive leaders. They have learned to get curious, to ask for help and to engage with their people. They sometimes then forget that their next step is to listen and to understand that their people may respond in different ways but that all must be equally valued.

Like most extroverts, I process my thinking externally. I talk as I think, and I have learned to process effectively in that way. However, what I had not understood was that by processing out loud, I was actually getting in the way of those who process internally. I was stealing all the processing time and not allowing them the space to reflect on my questions, digest them properly, make connections to information in their brains and then take time to articulate their own views. As a pleaser, problem solver and extrovert all in one, I was breaking all the rules of inclusion. It has taken a lot of practice for me to understand my impact and start giving space to others less like me. On my ongoing journey, I have learned to lean into being vulnerable and sharing with others that this is a blind spot for me and I have asked for accountability so that they can catch me when I trip up.

Silence is a beautiful gift that inclusive leaders can give their people. Get comfortable with pauses. Start to build thinking time into your team conversations. Hold back on your ideas and allow time for others to generate theirs.

 NUGGETS FOR REFLECTION AND ACTION

Reflect on and journal your responses to the following:

- How good are you at staying with silence and resisting the urge to fill the spaces?

- Who has enough exposure to you in conversations and could give you an honest rating on your success with this? Would you ask them to?

Slow down

Hand in hand with silence comes the need to slow down. This can be a real challenge given how much you probably need to juggle every day. Busyness has become our norm and we are often already at the next meeting in our heads before we have wrapped up the one in progress. While the world now seems to celebrate busyness, it creates additional problems for leaders who must ensure that, amid the busyness, they always retain the time and space to ensure that their people feel truly seen and heard. Without this, rapport and trust levels will suffer.

Pace can determine how inclusive you are and can affect how independent your people are with problem-solving. I am a huge advocate of Nancy Kline's 'time to think' process outlined in her book *Time to Think: Listening to Ignite the Human Mind.* In it, she summarises the value of pace brilliantly: 'Ease creates. Urgency destroys. When it comes to helping people think for themselves, sometimes doing means not doing.'[28]

In 2020, at the height of the surge in the Black Lives Matter (BLM) movement fuelled by the horrendous murder of George Floyd in May, I was invited to facilitate a conversation between an executive team and their Black Employees Network. Within a few minutes of kicking off the meeting, I found that I was being pulled into working at their pace. They were quick to jump from one agenda item to another and move on from people's comments; it became a race to ensure we covered the seemingly endless list of additional agenda items packed into the meeting! As soon as this dawned on me, I asked for a moment to share my realisation with them:

'I need to really slow down, so much that it may possibly annoy you. I feel pulled into your pace and need for speed, so I need to reset here. We're not going to connect to one another, this experience and this crucial topic in an effective way if we carry on at this pace. Let's pause, reflect on what's been shared so far and talk about what's going on for each one of you.'

Taking my advice, the pace slowed, leading to a powerful conversation which not only enriched our understanding of the topic being discussed, but also generated a much greater awareness of one another.

I liken this frenetic rush to what the experience might be like for a baby who is just being introduced to solid food after months of living off milk. As a parent (leader), you initially offer only a small spoonful of food, allowing time for the baby (your people) to really taste the new food (new learning or information) for the first time (letting them feel initial reactions and compare this new information to that which has gone before). Only if given the time and space to work through this process will they be able to get back to you with their considered and authentic opinions. A leader should undertake the same paced process when introducing new subjects to their people or listening to their diverse experiences.

By slowing down and allowing space within the BLM meeting, people were able to recall and share powerful experiences. It also left room for everyone to be engaged in coming up with ideas to move forward. At the end of the meeting, one of the executives openly thanked me for slowing them down, reflecting on how much more used to talking they were than listening and how invaluable the experience had been:

'In the last forty-five minutes, we have felt more connected as a community than ever and feel more like we're in this together. Without you here, we would have made eight decisions by now and then changed our minds on all of them after we've had time to think after the meeting.'

Emotions

A common driver for leaders rushing through conversations is their desire to run from emotions. Many struggle just with staying with their own emotions, let alone allowing space for others to be with theirs. Let's take crying as an example, one that often comes up in coaching sessions where clients describe beating themselves up for crying or for not being able to deal with a situation where someone else has burst into tears at work.

A few years after leaving corporate employment, I met an ex-boss for lunch, and we got talking about some of our most challenging experiences in the bank where we had worked together. To my surprise, he said he felt traumatised by a particular experience with me that he had never forgotten. He recalled a one-to-one meeting where he had informed me that although he had put my name forward for a promotion, I had not been shortlisted. I had burst into tears at the news. He recounted how he had frozen, unsure how to handle the situation – he couldn't wait to get out of the meeting room! We both laughed as I explained that, although the news had been disappointing at the time, I hadn't been devastated: 'I'm a crier – my kids would tell you that I cry at TV adverts! You really needn't have worried,' I assured him.

This exchange had clearly been particularly difficult for my ex-boss, and he had assumed that my reaction revealed that equal distress. Had he felt able to ask me what I needed as my tears began to flow, I would have just asked for a minute to let the emotion out and we would just have carried on with the meeting. As a leader, he could have taken the time earlier to get to know me properly, perhaps even asking me how I would want to handle difficult conversations were they ever to arise. I could have explained that I cry when overwhelmed and we would have both been better prepared for the emotions that such an exchange could invoke.

Nowadays, my clients and most people that I work with know that I'm OK with emotions, and for their sake and mine, I like to share this about myself. I cry when I feel upset or angry, and I feel much better after a minute to pull myself together. I explain that you can learn something about yourself if my emotions make you uncomfortable, and it can provide an opportunity for you to explore how to be with strong emotions. I sometimes describe my own journey as a natural pleaser who always wanted to save people when they got upset or displayed strong emotions. In my first coach training programme with The Co-Active Training Institute, I learned how important it is always to remember that those I coach do not need to be rescued and to hold that they are 'naturally creative, resourceful and whole'.[29] What a great lesson to remember, pleaser!

As an inclusive leader, you do not get to decide how best to take care of your people or when they should be rescued. If you feel challenged by their emotions and tempted to shut them down, try asking them what they need from you at that moment and learn to just be with them as needed. Embrace emotions and ensure that you do not fall into the trap of suggesting that emotion, or the expression of emotions, is somehow 'wrong' and to be feared and avoided. Reserve judgement and get curious about what information they carry. Emotions are a form of communication and make us human. Listening to the emotions of your people will let them teach you how to become the best leader for them.

Celebrate

Celebration is an area that often gets neglected in workplaces, yet it is crucial for building motivation and developing your confidence as an individual and a team. As a leader, you need to understand that your people want to be seen and acknowledged. As humans, we like recognition and we want to be celebrated for the work we do. Like most people, you are probably more likely to associate celebrations with personal milestones such as birthdays, graduations, etc; even at work, we tend to celebrate the big milestones such as promotions, company awards, etc. Where we find that leaders and teams struggle is in celebrating the day-to-day successes, particularly the small wins that come along on the journey to the big win.

I often pause midway through team coaching engagements to ask the teams to consider what they are celebrating about themselves. The reaction is almost always one of surprise as they take a moment to look at themselves as a team, to consider the journey they have been on together and to verbalise their team achievements. Most teams admit that this is something they never do, but they notice the energy grow in the room when they begin to share and celebrate their team success stories; many then commit to pushing themselves to celebrate more things, more often.

As humans, celebrating ourselves does not come naturally to us. In the process of scanning the environment for threats, our brains often turn inwards to search for what we have done wrong. Understanding that it is our default to be overly self-critical, we should learn to embrace celebrating ourselves and giving ourselves a metaphorical pat on the back. If you find this is struggle, this could be a signal that you still need to do some work on yourself. Think about and explore, perhaps with a coach, what has led you to resisting celebrations. How could you change those thoughts?

As an inclusive leader, learning to celebrate yourself and others is an invaluable gift to offer your people and you can model it by celebrating them and their achievements, no matter how small and inspiring. You should also encourage them to celebrate one another. There are opportunities for celebration everywhere once you have learned how and where to look!

 **Key lessons**

As an inclusive leader, you need to adapt your approach to leading your people by creating environments that motivate them to step forward as leaders themselves. You do that by:

- Bringing more vulnerability to your leadership

- Learning to take up less room, leaving more space for your people to think and contribute

- Building confidence by celebrating individual and collective successes

8
R – Reconnect

If you have been working through this book in order, you will now be getting ready to reset your leadership and start again with your team. You will be starting to look at the individuals in your team and in teams throughout the organisation through a different lens. You should now be ready to step into their worlds, reconnect, and in so doing, learn how to get the best out of them.

However, the journey so far will not have been just about others. You will also have been learning a lot about yourself, both through exploring your own thoughts and experiences in isolation, but also through the process of immersing yourself in and exploring the world of others – our relationships can be the most powerful mirrors and tools for our own self-discovery.

You understand that relationships must be nurtured. You are committed to inclusion and regularly seek to strengthen connections, with yourself, your team members and all those with whom you interact.

Mia joined the coaching session ready to jump right in. We had been working together for a few months and I always looked forward to our sessions. Mia was an engaged client and always came back prepared to share how she got on with her coaching 'homework'. She had already undergone significant changes from when we had first met.

Having previously worked on identifying her saboteur, today's task was a visualisation exercise designed to help her reconnect to her purpose and build motivation. By the end of the exercise, Mia had identified her own guru and personal hero, Sathya Sai Baba, the spiritual leader loved by Hindu and Muslim devotees throughout India and across the world. As our work together continued over the next few months, I came to learn more about Sai Baba and I noticed how Mia lit up whenever she spoke of him, her own love for Sai Baba inspired by her father's. She even told me that on her bucket list she had a plan to get a tattoo that symbolises her relationship with Sai Baba, but she had so far held back.

I started to wonder if this was the only way in which she held back from celebrating this key personal inspiration, so I became curious to find out how much her team members knew about Sai Baba. I was shocked to find that although images of Sai Baba were everything and everywhere for Mia – in her thoughts, her home and even in her car – she had never allowed herself to introduce this dominant part of herself at work. No wonder she felt she was different at work and somehow not truly herself. Through the coaching journey, Mia recognised that not bringing her authentic self to work was limiting her ability to show up authentically, her confidence and, ultimately, her performance.

Several weeks later, Mia appeared visibly excited in our session. 'Yes! I got that tattoo! My husband even got one too,' she exclaimed, as she raised her wrist to the camera to show a beautiful feather tattoo with the inscription, 'Sai Baba'.

'Mia, it is stunning, and I can see just how much it means to you,' I replied. The glow on her face was priceless. Mia then went on to describe the reception of her tattoo in the office. One of her colleagues who sat opposite had asked what made her get a tattoo, noting that this seemingly spontaneous act seemed so unlike her. Mia shared her story with her colleague, then with her boss who had made the same inquiry, and both times she found it had opened a really authentic and unguarded conversation about their true selves, making them feel much more strongly connected. Mia's story is a perfect illustration of the importance of creating inclusive workplaces where every individual can fully and authentically show up as themselves and thrive in doing so.

In this chapter, you will learn new ways to connect with your people. In forming these connections, not only will you get to know them better, but you will also let free new ways of thinking, inspire authentic leadership and shape an inclusive culture.

Love the past

As a leader, you will sometimes find yourself in situations where it feels far easier and better to press on and dictate how things should be done, rather than create time and space for others to show up fully in a way that works best for them, not as defined by you. Certainly, there will be times when you do need to get in the driver's seat and move things forward and moments when decisive leadership is required, but these moments are probably far fewer than you would tend to believe.

Whether you are a new leader or experienced, the inclusive leader understands that it is important to regularly stop and reflect on how far you have come, both individually and collectively with your people. There will be existing ways of working and being together in your workplaces that have helped you get to where you are today, but as you together undertake change, it is important to review these as you take on and embrace new ways. Decide which ways you will carry forward and then accept that you may need to let go of some that no longer serve you.

Some of these goodbyes will come with sadness, and you must understand that some people will need more time than others before they can let go. Forging ahead can seem appropriate and exciting in the short-term, but in the long-term many leaders and organisations find that they encounter much more resistance to change if the journey has not begun correctly. In our Change Management programmes, we find that people are most likely to struggle to embrace new ways when leaders have rushed to implement change and start working differently without allowing people time to reflect on, celebrate and then lay down the old ways that have got them to where they are today. We saw this play out as teams had no choice but to make an instant shift from office-based ways of working to virtual and then hybrid due to the pandemic.

Your existing habits have served you and your people well, but as you all grow and change, now is the moment to stop, review, revise and reconnect. Skipping this process and rushing into change can lead to a subconscious rejection of the new ways and possibilities and feed ongoing fantasising about the old ways. Allow time to reflect, process and mourn so that you can all let go in a way that serves the future more effectively.

 NUGGETS FOR REFLECTION AND ACTION

Consider a change that is impacting you or your team. Reflect on and journal your responses to the following questions:

- How have the old ways served you?
- Which ways should you now let go of?
- What will you miss about those old ways? Are there things that could make this parting easier?
- What would you like to hold on to and carry forward?

Ditch the job description

This phrase was the title of a blog post I published on LinkedIn, inspired by the experiences shared by several career change clients coached over the years. My post prompted a few messages from contacts who commented that the topic really resonated with them, and this then initiated some interesting conversations.

I decided to explore this further in a coaching session with a team client that had described feeling stale. I asked each of the team members to go away and write their own job descriptions based on the roles and responsibilities they have undertaken so far. They then shared these descriptions with their colleagues and invited a discussion. The session was incredibly insightful as the colleagues realised that they had made a lot of assumptions about each other's roles and responsibilities. It also sparked a conversation about unacknowledged contributions, duplication of efforts and the lack of systemised processes that left the team open to risk by retaining the details of processes and procedures just with individuals, rather than collectively. The team members acknowledged and recognised the pressures each member was under, exploring ways to support one another and develop newer and better ways of collaborating.

For the second part of the exercise, I asked the team members to put aside those roles and responsibilities, to put aside the job descriptions, and instead to explore their identities, considering the many different elements and influences that had made them the unique individuals they were now. This was when the connections sparked, as they began to recognise commonalities and differences, shared identities and experiences. Stripped of the job descriptions and labels, they truly saw and witnessed one another as they recognised useful team skills and talent that had been marginalised. This was another step to opening more possibilities, mutual support, co-creation and innovation.

Personally, I can't stand the weight and degree of significance placed on job descriptions. They can become unchallenged directives for what one should or should not do and be responsible for within the workplace. Along with strict job hierarchies in organisations, I believe job descriptions kill creativity and inhibit thinking outside the box. They force your diverse people to fit into your predetermined expectations and marginalise their contributions, suppressing the introduction of additional skills and talents that could serve your organisation well if only they were harnessed.

Co-design your team

When I look back over a decade of running my business, I am astounded to see how much the experience has stretched me. I have experienced at least ten times more growth and development than I would have done had I stayed in-house. In the process of trying out all aspects of running a business, I learned more about what I find exciting and identified areas where

I excel and those where I feel little stimulation. This all led to knowing myself better and designing my work in a way that enables me to add the most value to my clients while still loving my work.

You can facilitate similar growth and self-development with your people. Make an effort to meet your team members individually and try to get to know who they are as individuals beyond their job descriptions. Review Part One of this book and the self-leadership lessons and activities that you have undertaken, and then work through similar exercises with your team members. As they learn about themselves, explore with them how they would design their roles to best match their strengths and ambitions and consider how elements of this ideal role could be introduced today. Before our newest team member joined us, our operations lead and I spent time exploring aspects of her role that she loved and those that she was not so keen on. Of the ones she was happy to let go of, we looked at how we could revise them to be more suitable and then merged others into the ideal job requirements for the new role we advertised. Fortunately, we found the right candidate with great experience and desire for the new role.

You could do a similar one-to-one job analysis with your team members, or better still, challenge your team to a team event where together you explore how you could redesign your team to best serve and use the individuals within it, while still ensuring that all relevant responsibilities are covered. The results may surprise you all!

Meet your team

As leaders, we easily fall into the trap of conflating people's job role and their identity. In leadership, we have control over people's job roles, but we must never seek to control their identity. When we start out in leadership, we embrace this control, but over time, we can become addicted to it. This becomes a limitation when we get to the scale-up stage and need to loosen the reins or let go.

I once conducted an exit interview for a departing employee, Aruna. Her organisation was devastated by the loss of this top talent to the competition. In the interview, Aruna spoke about feeling constrained by her previous job and the team that she was in. She had shared her frustrations and ambitions with her boss but had seen no real efforts to explore other possibilities for her outside her role and the current team.

Aruna had found a mentor through a business network and started getting support. She described to me how the mentor took time to explore her dreams, worked with her on her five-year vision and then challenged her to explore all possible paths to making her dream a reality. Unfortunately, Aruna's previous disappointment with trying to speak to her manager led her now to believe that there was no point trying to explore her dreams within this organisation. Instead, her mentor helped her identify new possibilities elsewhere, facilitated introductions to others in his network, and consequently, helped her land an exciting new role with a competitor organisation. It was her organisation's loss. Had they heard her frustrations and explored her needs and aspirations, as the mentor did, they could have identified that there were already existing similar opportunities within their organisation, enabling them to retain her and harness her talent.

Dedicate time to having informal career development conversations with your people. Put aside the job titles and descriptions and focus instead on seeing the people, on helping them create opportunities that would excite them, engage them differently and help them be their best possible selves, even if that means a move outside your team to a different role within your organisation. An inclusive leader can see not just the forest, but also the individual trees within. They recognise that everyone is an asset to the entire organisation and do not let job expectations get in the way of creating opportunities that get the best out of their people.

Diversify possibilities

To reconnect with your people means allowing them space to show up, harness their diversity and co-create possibilities for your organisation. One way in which you can fuel creativity while building your people's independence and confidence is by offering them an opportunity to dedicate some of their work time to creating and owning a project.

In their 2004 Founders' Letter, Google founders Larry Page and Sergey Brin introduced their '20% project', which gave their people the option to dedicate 20% of their work time (effectively one full day per week) to work on a Google-related passion project of their own choosing or creation.[30] As Page and Brin explained, this project has resulted in 'many of our most significant advances', including products such as AdSense, Google News and Gmail, all originally prototyped through this project.

Although few companies have adopted anything quite as extensive as the '20% project' (and even at Google, uptake has dropped), other companies have reportedly offered variations of this benefit to their staff, including programmes such as InCubator at LinkedIn and Blue Sky at Apple. The outdoor retailer Patagonia often ranks highly on lists of the best place to work in America. They cite employee autonomy as one of the ways through which they achieve this ranking. Their variation sees employees setting their own work schedules to allow for better work-life balance and, consequently, employee engagement.[31] I find that many of the founders that I meet and work with have introduced variations of this form of autonomy and empowerment. It is such a great way to make creative space for your people, to enable their diversity of thinking, ideas and possibilities to blossom freely. One key here is that you must remain totally unattached and open to the outcome so that their freedom to think and explore is not restricted by your influence, intention or otherwise.

 NUGGETS FOR REFLECTION AND ACTION

Reflect on and journal your responses on how you could:

- Make a commitment to look at each team member through your new lens of inclusion.
- Reconnect with each team member and make space to harness their diversity and creativity, allowing them to influence the direction of your services, products or organisation.
- Dedicate time to career and team development conversations where you step back, let go of the need to drive and co-create possibilities.

Sense of belonging

The human brain has a need for a sense of belonging and the last few decades have seen an increased interest in the role of mirror neurons in this process. These are a particular class of neurons which fire in the brain when an individual acts, but also fire off in the same way if the individual observes the action performed by another; activity within the brain of the observer 'mirrors' the neuronal activity taking place within the brain of the one they observe. These neurons therefore play a crucial role in allowing us to empathise and imitate others and in increasing our understanding of the value of social connection, recognition and relatedness.

Research has long shown the importance of social connection for humans – we have a fundamental and instinctive need to belong and to feel connected to others. Research by Naomi Eisenberger has shown that '"social pain" – the painful feelings following social rejection or social loss' elicits the same neural response in the brain as physical pain.[32] We experience pain when we feel excluded and isolated from others. This triggers our threat response and leads to anxiety and stress.

We learned earlier how damaging this threat cycle can be, and as an inclusive leader, recognising this human tendency will be beneficial as you find ways to prioritise creating a sense of belonging and 'togetherness' among the diverse people in your teams. This can be hard: most organisational reward schemes and incentive practices are geared towards individual achievement, promoting competition and discouraging teamwork and collaboration. Unsurprisingly, team development is also often less of a focus for most teams, as leaders prioritise individual development needs. This often results in more demand for individual coaching than team coaching. Both forms of development are important, but leaders often recognise the need for both when it is too late. This is similar to couples relying on individual therapies to tackle relationship development needs and only resorting to couples therapies when things are at breaking point. Leaders can counteract this oversight by implementing practices that also cater for team needs, specifically rewarding and celebrating relationships, connection, inclusion and collaboration.

Learn to follow

You know yourself better than anyone else does; the same is true for your people. Leadership starts with knowing yourself, and only then can you move on to learning to understand your people. Do not assume that you already know the individuals in your team, what their career challenges are or how best to support them. Learn to step back, let go of leading others in the same way that you would like to be led, and seek their guidance on what works best for them. An inclusive leader regularly asks for feedback on the impact of their leadership and leans on their people to help them become leaders that effectively harness diversity. Letting go as an inclusive leader means being open, not just to sharing leadership, but to passing it on if there is need for a particular expertise which does not lie with you. Remember that perverse power inherent in displaying vulnerability that we learned about in Part One?

During the Covid-19 pandemic, as lockdown started to ease in various countries, I was asked at a leadership conference to advise leaders on how best to approach changing restrictions and expectations concerning mask-wearing, invitations to come back into the office and networking. I was surprised to hear that some leaders expected to make these decisions without consulting with their people or including them in the discussion about how best to proceed in a way that respects individual rights, but also protects others.

There will always be some decisions that you have to make and own alone as an inclusive leader. However, you will also find that there are some decisions – more than you might first think – where you can invite others to work with you on a decision. To engage in this collaborative decision-making, it is important that you first become totally clear on which areas are non-negotiable for you and that you are then transparent with your people about what makes them this way. Most importantly, you must ensure that you are truly open and receptive in these discussions, not just present in body but fixed in mind. You should listen to the opinions of others openly and without agenda and remain open to being swayed, influenced and led on decisions where appropriate.

When my elder daughter Adora was eight years old, she once taught me a valuable lesson. At the time, I was pondering how best to speak at a virtual event scheduled for a time when my children would still be running around the house and not yet ready for bedtime. She asked what was on my mind, so I decided to share my dilemma with her.

Me: I have a really important talk to give later, but as I'm the only adult in the house with you, I'm worried that I might get distracted by you and Abigail running around and interrupting me. If that happens, I won't be able to concentrate. I think I need help with how to make this work.

Adora: I can coach you!

Me: Oh, OK. That would be great.

Adora: [Thinks for a second before replying with a cheeky grin] Just ask me to be in charge and allow us, this once, to have treats and a movie on a school night. If you do, I promise that I will keep Abigail in our room and we won't distract you.

With her input and ideas, this was the problem solved and she later took her responsibility seriously. Why hadn't I thought of that?

NUGGETS FOR REFLECTION AND ACTION

Reflect on and journal your responses to the following:

- As a leader, where do you hold on to leadership and in doing so, limit opportunities for others to lead and develop as leaders too?
- Where are you not taking advantage of all that your team has to offer you?
- What is one action you can take this week as a first step to opening yourself up to influence from your people?

Share stories

One of the greatest missteps I see in leaders can be found in the stories they tell, how they tell them, and in some cases, if they tell them at all. Stories are one of the quickest ways to build connection and bring humanity to your leadership. By sharing your stories, you provide more opportunities for you and your people to find common ground and unite around shared experiences. We communicate so much more than we know through the stories we tell: our values, our ideas, our social rules and our behaviour patterns. We also build the strongest and most memorable legacies through our stories and the inspiration they provide and this helps us to leave our mark and be remembered.

At the start of this chapter we discussed Mia's journey as she learned to share her stories of Sai Baba. Throughout this book, I have also shared my own stories and experiences. I hope that some of them will have resonated with you and triggered memories of and reflection on your own experiences. By sharing your stories, and sharing more of yourself through them, you will inspire others to share more of themselves too. In turn, this will stimulate new ways for them to bring more of their authentic selves into your workplace, so that the true richness of your collective diversity can be harnessed.

 NUGGETS FOR REFLECTION AND ACTION

Take some time to reflect on who and what inspired your leadership journey. Reflect on and journal your responses to the following questions:

- What childhood experiences marked defining moments for you?

- Which three stories do you most often share when you talk about your leadership journey?

- What is the impact of each story on the listener? Do they help build connections and spark curiosity and creativity?

- If you cannot recall any stories previously shared, take some time to think about your own experience of, or journey to, authentic leadership. Use your experiences on this journey to craft some stories that you can share with others.

Motivation and reward

As we have already covered, our brains are constantly scanning the environment around us, assessing each new thing we encounter to gauge whether it is one we should go toward or one from which we should move away. Our behaviour is constantly influenced by the joint desire of the brain to maximise reward and minimise threat. This is thought to be a deeply primal survival instinct, but it is just as true in feedback situations.

In 2008, Dr David Rock, co-founder and CEO of the NeuroLeadership Institute, developed and shared his 'SCARF model'. He identifies what he considers to be five key domains in human experience, introduced by the acronym SCARF:

> 'Status is about relative importance to others. Certainty concerns being able to predict the future. Autonomy provides a sense of control over events. Relatedness is a sense of safety with others, of friend rather than foe. And Fairness is a perception of fair exchanges between people [emphasis added].'[33]

Understanding how these domains function together and interact to drive human social behaviour is key to inclusive leadership. While you can never really know what is going on for each of your team members – indeed, they may not even know themselves – understanding their possible motivations will enable you to better understand what drives them, what might trigger them and better predict likely outcomes or results to particular actions or approaches.

For instance, using the SCARF model and the joint drivers of threat and reward, let us consider the way feedback may be shared with, and received by, an individual. If the feedback recipient feels that any one or more of the five SCARF domains are being challenged, the feedback will likely be received as a threat and their behaviour in response will reflect this; the same is true if the feedback activates a reward response. Knowing this, you can develop and style your leadership accordingly. By understanding this delicate balance between threat and reward and how the domains outlined in the SCARF model can affect this, you can tailor how you lead your team members and learn how to work most effectively in a way that minimises perceived threats and maximises the positive feelings generated by reward.

 NUGGETS FOR REFLECTION AND ACTION

Reflect on and journal your responses to the following:

- To what extent do you know what motivates each of your team members?
- How does each one perceive 'career success'?
- If they were to get some autonomy to shape their role, what will they change, add or remove?

- How could that change benefit you as an organisation? Will you ask them?

🔆📖 Key lessons

To be an inclusive leader, you will need to step back or even let go to see your people through a different lens – one not defined by their roles and job titles. You can do this by:

- Accepting that change is needed to move you forward to being more inclusive

- Taking time to acknowledge and honour how your old ways of leadership have served you thus far, consciously choosing what to let go of and what to take on, and inviting your people to move forward with you

- Learning to open up to others more and sharing your own authentic stories and experiences so you can inspire others to do the same

- Engaging your people individually and collectively in designing how best you can lead them to get the best out of them

9
E – Empower

When you lead an empowered team, team members are aligned around a common vision and leadership is a hat that everyone can wear. There is collective commitment to continuous improvement, and you are all 'in it together'.

In previous chapters, emphasis has been on the changes that you need to make during your journey to letting go and becoming more inclusive. In this chapter, the focus is on how you relate differently to a team in a way that builds their confidence and motivates them to step up. Let's look at a team coaching experience that surfaced this need to a leader.

My colleague and I checked in at the conference centre where we were due to meet a senior leadership team for their second team coaching session. The first session had revealed a significant over-dependence by the team on their leader, Sofia. She was clearly a great leader: engagement within the team was high and they all stressed that she was extremely supportive. Hearing the team starting to discuss what I was beginning to recognise as their dependency, Sofia commented that she felt validated as she heard them acknowledging the huge volume of demands they had placed on her. She was excited about the second session and keen to start looking at how the team could now step up more and what support they would need from her to do this.

We began the session, and for one of the exercises, we asked team members to share individually the extent to which they considered they took ownership and responsibility for driving change within the team. As we had expected, most of them acknowledged it was little. To try and better understand the barriers they were experiencing, we then probed this further by using examples of opportunities where they could have stepped up but had chosen not to. It quickly became apparent that, although they had often wanted to step up, they had felt Sofia always had everything under control. Hearing this was obviously an 'aha' moment for Sofia. She saw how she had inadvertently been excluding others in her desperate attempt to hold everything together alone, and to her credit, she immediately confessed: 'My team doesn't need to step up; I need to step back!'

Over subsequent sessions, my team and I went on to work with Sofia through one-to-one leadership coaching, while also coaching her team to redesign their culture and embrace leadership as a shared opportunity and responsibility. The team gained confidence in knowing how and when to step up, and Sofia learned when to step out of their way. By stepping back, she was able to create better balance in her life and was then able to take on more strategic leadership activities which she had previously neglected due to time constraints.

So, how did Sofia empower her team and how can you as an inclusive leader do the same?

Psychological safety

The construct of 'team psychological safety' was first developed by organisational behavioural scientist Amy Edmondson of Harvard, who defined it as 'a shared belief held by members of a team that the team is safe for interpersonal risk-taking.'[34] If I were in a team with psychological safety, I would feel secure, safe and able to ask for help, take healthy risks and admit when I get things wrong, knowing that my leader and colleagues have my back. In a team, this confidence in a shared mutual respect and trust would result in everyone learning and growing well as a team, in turn improving individual performance and overall team results.

Psychological safety can only develop where there is space and the right culture to facilitate a mutual respect and trust in your team members towards one another and towards you as their leader. In teams that do not have strong relationships, we often find that team members do not challenge one another enough. If you lead such a team, you will notice that issues, concerns and reservations about changes you might be considering or even implementing are suppressed and brushed under the carpet, because people do not feel safe enough to be vulnerable or to get things wrong. Only by sharing issues and concerns can they be addressed so that you can move together in a much stronger way, much more aligned as a team in terms of where you're going.

In a lot of teams that we coach, we find that lack of psychological safety often results in poor decision-making. These teams find that they make decisions, but within a few months, those decisions that were supposed to be long-term end up being challenged too late in the process. This results in further changes, or worse still, abandoning the recently adopted changes. This can lead to frustration and conflict, and over time, have a knock-on effect on the team morale. If this sounds familiar, ask yourself whether your team has sufficient psychological safety to challenge one another freely and openly and think about how you can create a more inclusive culture where team members can express vulnerability, take risks and challenge one another without fear of damaging relationships.

Stay out of it

One of the common ways that leaders disempower relationships within the teams is by permitting and even engaging in triangulation. According to an article by *Psychology Today*, 'Triangulation occurs when two people who are involved in a conflict attempt to involve a third party.'[35] This may be an attempt by one of the people or parties to draw reinforcement and support, and to retain control. While triangulation may occur through good intentions, such as to avoid conflict and deflect, it can result in great divisions between teams and unhealthy patterns of unspoken dynamics and tensions.

In a three-way contracting conversation with a new client and his boss (the coaching engagement sponsor), my client described learning that his colleagues had made complaints about him to his boss. He was resentful that his colleagues had chosen to enlist a third party – their boss – rather than first attempting to speak to him directly to resolve the complaints. It was clear that these indirect conversations had generated a lot of tension, as my client described a strong mistrust for his colleagues and his boss, and a general suspicion of being disliked and undervalued by those around him. This is the danger of triangulation.

As a leader, look out for triangulation patterns and try to reduce the frequency where it occurs. You may well come across situations where people try to draw you into their conflict. Resist the urge to get involved as you could inadvertently take sides, marginalise the other party or diminish their sense of belonging and feelings of fairness. To stay inclusive, here is what I recommend you do when presented with that dilemma:

- Try to reduce the frequency of triangulation communication patterns by recognising it where it occurs and actively taking steps to close it down.

- If you are approached as the third party, try to avoid getting drawn into engaging directly. Be clear about your boundaries. Avoid triangulation and dependency on you by instead taking this opportunity to coach them to develop confidence in their own ability to manage the situation directly and to have the necessary conversations.

- Find out from the person that approached you what support they need from you to help them to have that conversation. Ask them how you could help prepare them to approach the conversation constructively.

- Be aware of the possible impact of the forthcoming conversation with the recipient and look out for signs that they may also now need your support as their leader.

- If the two parties are unable to have that conversation on a one-to-one basis, offer to bring them together and to facilitate that conversation. In the interest of transparency and building trust within your team, ensure all conversations take place with both parties together in a room. Your role is not to take over in the conversations that they need to have, but to facilitate or mediate.

 NUGGETS FOR REFLECTION AND ACTION

Reflect on and journal your responses to the following.

If you find yourself tempted to get drawn into triangulation tropes and tend to step in to have team member conversations for them or on their behalf:

- Go back to your leadership archetype and explore how your desire to rescue, lead and problem-solve could be getting in the way of sharing leadership in this situation.

- Where else does this desire get in the way of you being inclusive?

- What steps will you take to ensure this desire does not limit inclusion?

To empower your people means letting go of the need to always be the one with the answers. This is particularly challenging for leaders who fall under the perfectionist, commander and problem solver archetypes. It requires you to become comfortable with not getting involved. You must also accept that your decisions will sometimes be challenged and even overturned as your people become more familiar with taking up space in your team and organisation.

Invite objections

One way to build skill in dealing with being challenged is to practise every day. It is good to engage your people in training you to become more open to being challenged. In the process, you will be developing your people's confidence and ability to challenge you.

Here is a great tip that I often give leaders who complain about their teams being too dependent on them and too passive in making decisions or taking leadership (in addition to not voting so readily, as covered in Chapter 7).

Invite dissent via a 'devil's advocate' into your regular meetings. Remember the three meeting roles covered in Chapter 7? If you would like to build in more challenges from your team members, try introducing a fourth role into any meeting that requires decision-making. This additional role will be the devil's advocate: 'a person who expresses a contentious opinion or adopts a particular stance chiefly in order to provoke debate or test the strength of the opposing arguments'.[36]

Like each of the other meeting roles, alternate who steps into it for each meeting. Explain that their task is to identify all possible reasons a potential course of action will not work. Remind the team to take the role lightly and to remember that it is nothing more than an assumed position for a particular purpose. Used correctly, the introduction of a devil's advocate can be a great risk mitigation process! While it may feel strange initially, I find that when teams go through this process effectively, they tend to identify a large number of potential risks, and as a result, can create a much stronger risk mitigation plan which really does come in handy when the teething problems of new initiatives start to emerge.

As your people get more comfortable with challenging you and each other, be aware of how that might trigger you, and where you might find yourself making judgements or being defensive, and allow yourself to embrace diverse views. This is a learning process for you and if you remain curious, you will come to recognise in yourself beliefs, attitudes or perceptions that you may need to unlearn to become more inclusive. Practise correcting, challenging and reframing these thoughts where they are unhelpful. For example, 'The non-conforming staff member who questions everything is not challenging me personally – they are invaluable to me as they ensure that decisions are well thought through and that we are prepared for any objections from the outside.' Understanding and embracing this fully will, with time and practice, become totally embedded in your inclusive leadership.

Rebrand conflict

In our Seek Feedback stage, when we invite team members to assess their team performance, we often find that there is an issue around stifled creativity and innovation. We find that conflict, or the lack of it, often gets in the way of teams being truly creative and innovative and prevents getting the best out of team members. Over the years, I have become an advocate for conflict and have trained countless teams to learn to disagree with and challenge one another constructively.

Yes, I do love conflict! I love it because it has a bad reputation and yet, when it's done properly, it can be a powerful tool. An inclusive leader shapes a team culture and builds teams that have enough trust, connection, vulnerability and safety in the relationships to allow members to question, challenge and disagree with one another. These teams can do conflict in a way that is healthy and without a fear of damaging relationships. It is in this muddiness of conflict that the gift that diversity offers can often be unlocked.

 NUGGETS FOR REFLECTION AND ACTION

Reflect on and journal your responses to the following:

- Is your team one in which people tend to agree to things not because they necessarily agree, but because they'd rather avoid conflict? Do they worry that disagreeing risks damaging relationships or triggering someone or one another?

- Is your team's identity and culture a true reflection of the diversity within it, or is it predominantly influenced by you?

Decide together

As an inclusive leader, it is your responsibility to ensure that you have built up enough trust in relationships between team members that they feel able to challenge one another, speak up about uncertainties and ensure alignment in ways forward.

Ineffective decision-making is often identified as a development need when we first assess teams on what keeps them 'playing small' or holds them back. When we dig deeper, it is almost always because team members are not sufficiently trained or equipped to challenge one another constructively, particularly at key moments when decisions are being made. This means that concerns and reservations are often suppressed and ignored. Too often this then results in poor decisions being allowed to go ahead where they could easily have been avoided if people had felt confident enough to speak up.

In a meeting between a new executive coaching client, his boss and me, I asked the boss how he envisaged the ideal relationship with my client. His answer was not what either of us had expected: 'What I really need from him is to know that he has my back.' Puzzled, I asked:

'And what would that look like?'

'It would mean that I would trust that he would always speak up when he saw me potentially making a wrong move. That would give me more confidence in my decisions and in him, and we could become trusted advisers to each other.'

What an empowering desire to share! Leaders, your most important team member is not the one who goes along with everything you say. It is the one who:

- Asks the questions that challenge you constructively

- Forces you to pause and think before you act

This person that readily takes on the devil's advocate role in your interactions will become a huge asset for your leadership and your team. Beware the desire to marginalise it because of a desire to avoid conflict, as that will do you all a disservice. They occupy that role because it is needed. It is one that every team ought to encourage and nurture!

 NUGGETS FOR REFLECTION AND ACTION

Reflect on and journal your responses to the following:

- Which voices do you pay more attention to in your team?
- When did you last acknowledge and reward the contributions of those who disagree with you?

- Which voice do you tend to disagree with? What value does that voice bring to your team? Challenge yourself to explore that voice with less judgement and more curiosity about what it has to offer.

Kill favouritism

When you marginalise those who are less like you or the others, you will begin to lean in and subconsciously support some team members more than others. Be aware that your archetype will also influence how and where you display this inadvertent favouritism.

Take Nisha, one of my leadership coaching clients, who described how she spent half an hour every morning with Mike, one of her direct report employees. Mike had developed an unhealthy dependency on Nisha and was now receiving significantly more of her time than the others within the team. When we analysed exactly what support Nisha was offering Mike, it became apparent that the learning and development that he was receiving from these one-to-one calls would be just as valuable for other members of her team. In the next team coaching session, we discussed Nisha offering coaching more broadly and the idea was warmly welcomed. A couple of team members spoke out, describing how they had been feeling resentment and jealousy towards Mike. They had concluded that Mike was Nisha's favourite, and it had never occurred to them that it could have been because he needed more support from her. Nisha had left an information gap and her employees had sought to fill it – as we have learned humans always will – but they had concluded incorrectly, and in doing so, tensions and division had developed. This is yet another example of the importance of being transparent with your people! Through my coaching, Nisha had shared with her team the challenge of how best to support all equally and had then stepped back, enabling the whole team to get involved in coming up with ideas and creative ways to develop and lean on one another.

Teacher's pet

We all know that one team member that seems to dedicate a lot of time to just being the 'teacher's pet'. To grow that closeness, they might be self-appointed whistle-blowers and tell-tales, voluntarily grassing on others and exposing those who may not be pulling their weight. These individuals are often hardworking and productive members of the team, but they lack self-confidence and so struggle to build strong, trusting relationships with their colleagues. You may find that you value and benefit from their input and the secrets they share with you, but as a leader, this could inadvertently reward and encourage toxic behaviours that impact on their ability to build and develop strong relationships with their peers. This is also another instance which presents a risk of you appearing to display favouritism. In turn, this can alienate other team members, erode trust in the team as a whole and create a culture that certainly cannot nurture a high-performing team.

In our team development programmes, one of the issues that we work with clients on at the Adapt phase is collaboration and mutual support. We often find that teams that score low in these areas are the least engaged and that is no surprise. Sometimes we find that the reason that they struggle with this is because they have a leader who falls into the hero or pleaser archetype. These leaders struggle to stay neutral when team members need them to; they may take sides, displaying it through their body language and other subtle signs even if their position is not verbalised. In doing that, they shape a culture where some members feel a strong sense of belonging while others struggle. It is your responsibility as an inclusive leader to ensure that every team member feels equally valued and respected and with a strong sense of rightful belonging in your team.

 NUGGETS FOR REFLECTION AND ACTION

Take some time to think about each one of your team members. Reflect on and journal your responses to the following questions:

- Who do you give more attention to than others?

- How does that impact on other team members and your team culture?
- To what extent do you help your team members to build strong relationships and work better together?
- Where do you display favouritism and how does that feed toxic behaviours or strain relationships in your team?

Prioritise equity

This moves us nicely to the need to maintain equity as an inclusive leader. Let's start with the definition of equity: 'The quality of being equal or fair; fairness, impartiality; even-handed dealing'.[37] You cannot be an inclusive leader without a continual, sharp focus on equity. It is important to consider the history of inequality if one is to do justice to this topic and that would take a whole new book. For now, let's look at racism as an example.

Following the horrendous murder of George Floyd in May 2020, the BLM movement took on a remarkable level of recognition globally. My colleagues and I spent a significant amount of time developing organisations which had finally resolved (some might say were forced) to start the work of becoming actively antiracist. This was a difficult journey with our clients. Not only did it further highlight the level of inequality and abuse that black people still have to face in the workplace, but I was also struck by just how much it took out of me as a black woman of mixed heritage compared to my white colleagues involved in the same work. Not only did I have to relive my own experiences of racism in the workplace, but I had to set aside some of those personal triggers to support internal diversity and inclusion (D&I) consultants while we listened to painful recounts of black people's experiences in today's workplace. As a black woman, I was still having to work harder than others and contribute more in emotional labour, even as we worked towards addressing racism and black inequality. There was a clear lack of equity even as we worked to address inequality. This is an often unacknowledged and neglected pain that many employees that run or play active roles in their organisations' employee network groups have to endure, with little or no support, recognition or reward.

 NUGGETS FOR REFLECTION AND ACTION

Consider the experiences of minority groups that you do not belong to. Reflect on and journal your responses to the following questions:

- What might it be like for them to navigate your organisation? Would they feel that they belong and are fully welcomed in your organisation?

- Are there any minority groups that you think might experience more problems within your organisation than others? Why is that?

- Your organisation was probably built based on the needs of those with privilege; how should it now change?
- How could you better engage, champion and sponsor your internal diversity, equity and inclusion experts and employee network groups?

Use your privileges

One of the uncomfortable inner places that I had to go to in preparation for doing antiracism work with organisations was to understand my own privileges, as well as those of others. As a woman, in many situations I am less privileged than the men around me. As a black woman, if I were in your organisation and it is predominantly white (like every organisation I have worked in to date), I am also less privileged than white women in your organisation. So I would benefit from women in leadership programmes that you may offer, but I would also have additional challenges and benefit from support for needs which would be unique to me as a black woman. Inclusive leadership requires constant curiosity and learning of these types of intersection. On the other hand, as an external consultant employed independently by organisations, I have the privilege of being able to share feedback, observations and recommendations derived from my interviews and focus group sessions with their diverse people without the same fear of repercussions or recriminations that employed members of staff might face. This is intersectionality, the idea that social organisation is composed of multiple different, overlapping and interconnected systems of privilege and power. No individual exists within a single social category, and we may hold varying positions of power versus discrimination in each of them.

When I work with organisations, one of the reasons I am able to identify, expose and share impactful feedback from their employees is because I can share my results truthfully and free of regulation or self-censorship. I have this freedom because, as a company director rather than an employee, I do not financially rely on one client. This is my privilege and my power, and as a coach, I have chosen to take on the responsibility to try and share this privilege. My focus group participants from minority groups often say that they love our sessions because they come in knowing that it will be a risk-free space and time in which they are safe to think and speak truthfully and unconstrained. My aim is to replicate, to some degree, the privilege afforded to me in my interactions with the organisation and the freedom that this privilege affords me. Our safe space empowers them to address issues and conversations that may have felt too dangerous in the wider organisation where fears for their interpersonal relationships, their status within the team and even their jobs result in self-censorship, unproductive and repetitive conversations and prevent the truth from getting spoken often enough.

As individuals, we each have different experiences of discrimination and oppression within a vast range of categories that impact on our personal, social and political identifies. You must learn to recognise these various power dynamics within your people, understand how they change moment to moment and seek always to support and elevate those who may be more marginalised or disempowered in any situation. As a leader, you hold great power over your people, and it is worth remembering that this is a privilege which your people do not hold. To be an inclusive leader, you must ensure that you always remember and acknowledge the privilege afforded by your position. You should be fully committed to constantly scanning how you use that power, searching to see if there are ways in which it could be more fairly distributed and making sure that you never abuse it!

 NUGGETS FOR REFLECTION AND ACTION

Reflect on and journal your responses to the following:

- Who within your organisation holds greater privilege and how does that allow them to progress?

- How can you, as an inclusive leader, redress the power imbalances within your organisation and ensure that your people all have equal opportunities? (Remember that this may not be about just giving equal access to the same opportunities. Equity is about recognising those intersectional dynamics at play and providing

> everyone with the support and resources they need to achieve an equal access to these opportunities.)

- How uncomfortable are you willing to be, what sacrifices are you willing to make and where could you cede power in service of inclusion?

Find sponsors

To empower your people and the relationships within your organisation, you need to ensure that you have an inclusive culture that creates the ground conditions necessary for everyone to feel supported, motivated to engage and confident that they can thrive. If you have paid close attention and reflected on the nuggets this book has offered, you will by now recognise that there is inequality in the workplace. You know that some groups of people have more privileges than others. Part of redressing that balance requires understanding the need for sponsorship that goes beyond mentoring. So what's the difference between mentoring and sponsorship?

A mentor is someone who offers you guidance, advice and support to help you achieve your goals; they are often already where you want to be in your career, experience or qualifications. In contrast, a sponsor is someone that has the privilege of a higher position and influence and who is committed to using their greater power to advance your career by giving you access to high-profile people, assignments and advancement opportunities. Where the mentor helps you gain the tools to work towards power yourself, the sponsor proactively uses their privilege and power to advance your progression. Inclusive leaders proactively facilitate sponsorship for their diverse people. As a leader on this journey to become inclusive, it is important that you acknowledge your privileges and prioritise connecting those who need it most with sponsors that will work with you to ensure a fair access to opportunities for all.

 NUGGETS FOR REFLECTION AND ACTION

Reflect on and journal your responses to the following:

- When you look at your senior leadership level, is it a reflection of your overall diverse population or are there populations that you see reflected across the organisations but which do not make it to the top?

- What gets in their way? How can you motivate those in the more privileged leadership roles to recognise the need for inclusion and offer sponsorship to those that most need it?

Wheel of Empowered Teams

If you have walked through this SHARE Leadership journey with your people, you will have a team with a shared vision and purpose that has moved on from being dependent on you to becoming empowered.

There will be healthy relationships between team members, and you will see that they draw from one another's leadership too.

To sustain shared leadership, your team will need to be empowered. To help you consider the extent to which your team is empowered, I have shared my Wheel of Empowered Teams below.

With a shared vision and purpose and an inclusive leader, a team will feel empowered if it has the following qualities:

- Clarity on roles and responsibilities, with team members knowing what is expected of them and where they would hold one another accountable

- A culture that allows team members to challenge one another constructively, fuelling creativity in their work and often generating further exciting ideas, inspiration and opportunities for collaboration

- Closer connections as people begin to work together more and tackle challenges as a team, even in disagreements and conflict

- Better communication with silos having been broken down, and regular feedback sought and embraced as relationships get stronger and stronger

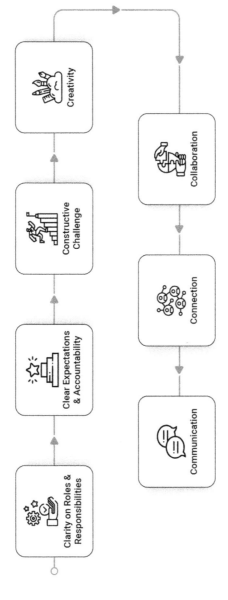

The Qualities of an Empowered Team

- A culture that allows its members to cycle through the wheel smoothly and consistently, ensuring everyone feels like they are in it together, through the good and tough times

The following exercise will help you to reflect on how empowered your teams are.

Think about a team that you lead. Using a scale of 1–10, mark how you would score your team on each of the seven qualities of empowered teams on the Wheel of Empowered Teams spidergram below. The eight sections represent different qualities present in teams that are empowered. The 'Other' segment has been left blank to give you an opportunity to include one other factor that you consider necessary for the team to be empowered.

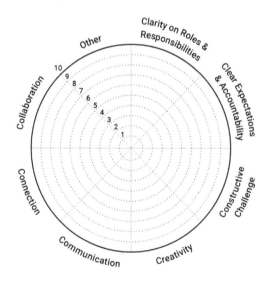

The Wheel of Empowered Teams

Using the centre of the wheel as 1 and the outer edges as 10, rank your level of satisfaction with each quality by drawing a line to create an edge for that section (see the example below).

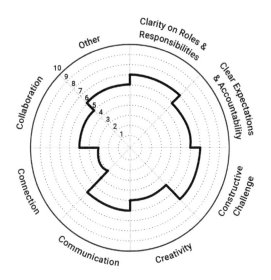

Example of the Completed Wheel

Do this exercise as the leader and then invite your team to complete a wheel with you too. How does your assessment of how empowered your team is compare to your team's assessment? Are there any surprises?

This exercise should prompt a conversation about what the team needs to feel more empowered. Refer back to the rating process covered in Chapter Six on Measures. For each quality, discuss what would be happening in the team for it to be rated a 10/10 on each quality. Agree some actions that would strengthen your team's rating against the qualities you would like to develop. Do not forget to build in being clear on roles and responsibilities, and accountability.

SHARE Leadership in practice

Let us use the triangulation challenge to practise using the SHARE Leadership approach to support a team member who has come to you to complain about another team member:

1. **Seek feedback:** Invite them to talk about their experiences and really listen, reserving judgement.

2. **Have accountability:** As you support the team member to prepare for the conversation they need to have with their colleague, consider how you could hold them accountable for having this conversation. Agree on a date by which the conversation will take place and how they plan to let you know once it has happened.

3. **Adapt:** Through your coaching, the team member will have more clarity on what they need to do and will be motivated to independently take control of the situation, knowing that you are there for them if they get stuck. There will be opportunity for them to develop or strengthen

their feedback and conflict management skills here.

4. **Reconnect:** As agreed, check in with them to explore the impact of the conversation after it has taken place. What lessons have they learned? What would they do differently if they come across similar challenges?

5. **Empower:** How can you support their ongoing development in relationship building and conflict management? What development needs have they surfaced because of this experience – individually and for your team as a whole? What training, coaching or developmental support could help strengthen your team's confidence and ability to have tough conversations, strengthen relationships and effectively manage conflict?

 NUGGETS FOR REFLECTION AND ACTION

Reflect on and journal your responses to the following:

- Refer back to the tendencies of the archetype that you most identified with. How would your archetype influence how you would have handled the above scenario?

- What are you learning about your tendencies and how they can derail inclusion and opportunities to empower your team?

- How will you remind yourself to let go when you find yourself in these situations that would tempt you to jump in?

 **Key lessons**

In this chapter, you have considered how you relate to and engage your people in leadership. You have learned ways to put the SHARE Leadership method into practice so that your people will develop the confidence and motivation to bring in the wisdom, creativity and innovation that their diversity can offer.

As the leader:

- Don't just delegate – empower. Don't just distribute tasks while still holding on to the responsibility and authority; equip your people with the skills and confidence they need to take ownership while you support from behind.

- When approached for support, know when to hold back on how you would handle situations. Ask more questions and learn to say, 'I don't know,' or, 'I would rather not vote.' Rather than expecting yourself to know everything and lead flawlessly, asking team members for help will build their own confidence and help them identify their own development needs. It will also give them permission to not know, to ask for help and to learn and develop their problem-solving skills.

- Find out what motivates your team members and facilitate opportunities for them to do what they love. Create time and space for side projects where possible, so that passion and creativity can thrive. Link side projects to motivation and you will find that engagement shoots up across the board.

- Commit to building strong relationships between your team members. That means encouraging them to lean on one another, not just you.

- Before jumping in to lead, first stop and consider if this is an opportunity to empower your team members. Coach individuals to find solutions to challenges they present to you. Where they are unable to do this alone, consider which of their colleagues could help. Encourage collaboration and connection within the team, generating independence from you and a shared responsibility.

PART THREE
SUSTAIN LEADERSHIP

In Part Two of this book, you learned that as an inclusive leader it is important to seek feedback, have accountability, adapt, reconnect and empower your people.

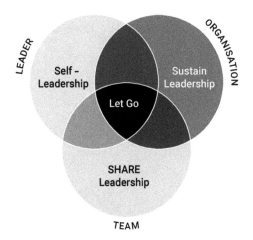

In this third part of the book, you will learn how to future-proof yourself as an inclusive leader by exploring ways to further let go and sustain shared leadership.

This will ensure that you will not be tempted to fall back into old leadership behaviours that exclude others and create a dependency on you.

10
Now What?

If you have been actively following this book's lessons and tips, you will have noticed that time and time again, your saboteur voice became incredibly loud. This is totally normal and should be expected. Remember that the job of the saboteur is to hold you down, suppress ambition and resist change.

Blame is your defensiveness

Be aware that the process of becoming an inclusive leader is always ongoing. Your saboteur will not disappear but will instead keep popping up here and there to remind you of all the reasons why you should revert to your old, limiting ways of leadership. You will feel like you do not have time to undertake the work necessary to become inclusive. You will start to stress that you do not yet have the right team to begin sharing your leadership and first need to recruit. You will blame processes and systems within your organisation for not making room for you to let go and be inclusive. You will find these reasons, and so many more, that will feel as though they stand in your way.

Here is my invitation to you: allow yourself to hear these reasons and write them down. Think about how they mask your defensiveness. What information do they have to offer you on where you need to stretch and let go? What do they tell you about your feelings towards others and towards change? Act to turn each of your reasons into a constructive challenge and start to work through them in turn, taking small steps every day. Your coach, trusted adviser or accountability buddy can help you in this work too.

Here is an example of a leadership team that successfully did this and was then able to flip their blame, capture their defensiveness, develop the awareness they needed and positively act.

I was coaching this team a few years ago and they were lamenting the stress caused by a particular team member who was absent from our session that day. He was widely seen as 'disgruntled' and one team member even referred to him as a 'bad apple'. That was the trigger that I needed to challenge them. My clients expect this from me and know that I firmly believe that there is no point in them investing in coaching if all it does is provide space to keep circling around the same old conversations that they are good at having! I asked a few questions:

'Has anybody provided any direct feedback to this colleague?'

No response.

'What does that say about this team, that you are talking about one of your own behind their back but without having given him any feedback or opportunities to change'?

Silence.

'Were this colleague to leave, which of you can say with certainty that the issues you blame him for would disappear?'

Yes, you guessed right – no one.

'Who would agree with me that, if you had the right team culture, behaviour like that of your colleague would not be able to survive, let alone thrive?'

They all agreed.

This was the moment they got ready to do the work. They now recognised that the behaviour that team member was exhibiting was just a symptom, an expression of their collective culture. If he left, they would have lost the opportunity to learn from the information and opportunities for team development that he was offering them. They left our session with a solid plan and committed to address the root cause of their challenges within the team: a generalised lack of feedback, mutual support and collaboration.

Pay attention to the damage that blame can cause to your cohesion as a team, as well as to your progression as an inclusive leader. When you next catch yourself pointing fingers, consider where that behaviour might be masking your defensiveness and get curious about what lesson you need to learn.

Sphere of influence

As a leader, you need to recognise that this journey towards inclusivity is a learning process that requires mindfulness, patience and self-care. Part of this process is becoming clear on what lies within your control or influence, knowing when to enlist others and to seek help. Patience and your commitment to this life-long journey of inclusive leadership is key.

Your ability to make change, and how fast you do it, depend to some degree on your degree of influence within your organisation. A CEO who is able to work free from ongoing oversight, input and interference from their board is likely to have a large degree of influence and the ability to make significant changes to processes and systems within the organisation, within a short amount of time. By contrast, a new leader might find they have to jump through many more hoops to get sufficient support to bring about change and it might feel like it takes forever. Whatever your degree of influence and control, make a commitment to use it to shape a more inclusive culture across your organisation and to empower those who may feel they have little influence or control.

It is also important to recognise areas outside your control. Identify these areas and think about whether it is necessary for you to have control or influence in these areas, or whether they are better handed to others? How can you best influence those that have more control on those areas than you to achieve the preferred outcome? Acknowledge that the path will not always be smooth. You are bound to come across obstacles and resistance. Planning how to tackle these when they arise, ensuring you have agreement and support from those around you, and building in some accountability will help you keep focused on what is within your control and prevent your saboteur from derailing you. You will need to keep building this resilience as you continue to recognise the privileges that leadership affords you, and increasingly use those privileges in service of those who are without. As you develop this awareness, do not forget to share your learning with your people and invite them to develop too.

Letting go

Let's explore how leaders unnecessarily holding on to power often results in complaints of insufficient time to share leadership.

I once challenged a senior leader who complained about how little time she felt she had to work on expanding her network and engaging in more strategic activities. She believed that this was because she did not have the right people in her team to support her appropriately. As part of her coaching exercises, I asked her to make a list of all the activities that took up her time. As the list got longer and longer, it became clear to me that she was right – she had no time to be the senior leader that her role required her to be!

My client identified that she had the tendencies of a protector archetype, and her choices and actions were heavily influenced by a need to guard others. She was so keen to avoid risking overwhelming her direct reports that she had not yet been able to let go of her old role effectively, despite not yet being where she could be – and needed to be – in her new one. She was stifling her own progression in service of those that worked for her, or so she felt. In her drive to become what she understood as a truly supportive leader, she was also stifling others. The individuals that she was supporting were not being empowered, nor was she leaving them sufficient space to develop and build new skills. Ultimately, this also stalled the organisation, as she was not equipping it for sustainable success in her absence. In our coaching, we needed to develop her skill of letting go so she was free to seize the better and more suitable opportunities now available to her. The organisation also needed to stretch and grow, encouraging middle management to do the same!

I introduced her to the following tool to help her audit her tasks and assess her time-management.

This task-focused process can help you not only share leadership but to develop your team. Track how you spend your working hours for two weeks. Make a list of everything that takes up your time. Consider the following audit questions:

- Which tasks or activities could be passed on to others?

- Which task(s) could provide a development opportunity for one of my team members? A good one to pass on to someone in your team to learn could be the skill that you've already successfully developed. You can now take on a coaching or supervisory role to help them build expertise and confidence in the new skill.

- Which task(s) could benefit from more diverse thinking, input and creativity from your team?

Now do the same for your meetings. Look at your calendar for the coming week and ask yourself:

- Which meeting(s) absolutely need me to be present?

- Which meeting(s) could provide an opportunity for a team member to step up, either to join me at the meeting, or to attend on my behalf?

As my client worked through the task, she began to see that, in her desire to rescue and protect her people, she had also been missing many opportunities for developing her team, and this had held them back from progressing. Time was available for appropriate development and progression for all if only she could step back, let go and trust her people more.

 NUGGETS FOR REFLECTION AND ACTION

Reflect on and journal your responses to the following:

- Your responses to the audit questions.
- To make lasting and sustainable change, try going through the audit questions at the end of each week or as you prepare for the following week's meetings and activities and track your progress in learning to let go.

Legacy matters

As you become more inclusive, you will also begin to shape your legacy and the story your people will tell of your leadership impact, today and in the future.

I recently had a conversation with one of my ex-bosses, Sunni from Morgan Stanley. Even though it had been over fifteen years since I had reported to her, we had stayed in touch and become good friends over the years. Just before calling Sunni, I had spent some time raving about her to another future leader. On the call with Sunni that followed, I found myself telling her what I had loved about her leadership, the impact she had had on me and how her legacy still lives on in me and my work in leadership:

'You are one of the most humble, loving leaders of my career, with an ability to balance the right amount of constructive challenge with motivation and inspiration to excel. You taught me so much about authentic and generous leadership.'

Even though embarrassed by my effusive praise, Sunni clearly cherished my words and valued hearing my acknowledgement of her impact. Through my recollections, I was testifying to her positive legacy and the profound impression she had left on me and those I now lead. What about you? What would your current team members say to you about your legacy?

NUGGETS FOR REFLECTION AND ACTION

Reflect on and journal your responses to the following:

- Think about yourself as a leader and think about what the people that you lead today will say about you and your leadership five, ten, twenty years from now?

- To what extent will you have motivated them to show up authentically, to celebrate their diversity and to bring those differences into shaping an inclusive culture within your organisation?

- Where do you still have work to do to secure a positive legacy of inclusion?

Your celebration bank

On your journey towards becoming more inclusive, you will have learned many things; however, there will also be things for you to unlearn. Personally, I have had to unlearn a lot to embrace, celebrate and harness my own diversity and my unique potential. Through this unlearning process, I have come to understand the value of rethinking belief systems that have influenced how we show up in the world.

Let us consider an example of this 'unlearning' process. When I facilitate leadership development workshops for multicultural networks, I often speak about the importance of exposure and visibility for career development. I also share one of my father's life lessons and describe how I have had to reframe and unlearn it to excel. I was a confident child and, fearing that I could grow up arrogant, my dad often cautioned me – 'Don't blow your own trumpet' – to warn me of the dangers of self-promotion and excessive pride when I tried to boast of one of my many achievements as a child. Decades later, I had to challenge and unlearn this widely accepted idiom. To progress up the corporate ladder, particularly as a black woman, it was fundamentally important that my work was widely known and talked about, but the only way to ensure this visibility was to proactively promote myself and my work. Without learning to blow my own trumpet, my successes in the corporate world, and more recently as a business founder, would have been limited.

I still struggle sometimes to own my worth and to recognise how good I am at what I do. When my saboteur voice grows loud, I remind myself that I will excel at whatever I put my mind to, whatever life may throw at me.

That's where my celebration bank comes in handy. A celebration bank is a dedicated space where you house all positive feedback, testimonials, emails, exchanges or thoughts that make you feel good about yourself. It can come in the form of a physical space such as an archive box or notebook, or a virtual space such as an email folder, online archive or even your LinkedIn profile. Here I collate testimonials, recommendations and record great things people have said about me and my impact. It is my secret weapon for those moments when my saboteur starts screaming at me, when I struggle to blow my own trumpet, or when my confidence gets knocked.

As an inclusive leader who is sharing leadership, you will almost certainly also face these moments of self-doubt. These are the times when your saboteur would have you question what value you add as you grow and empower others to lead, and you may find yourself tempted to draw back to your place of safety, grabbing on to leadership once again and holding on far too tightly.

It is hard to let go of activities that lie in your comfort zone at these times. This is the point to reach into your celebration bank of positivity and draw from it to remind yourself to celebrate your journey so far, the impact you have on others and the difference you make as a leader committed to inclusion. In this way you can silence the saboteur and move forward renewed with ambition and confidence once again.

 NUGGETS FOR REFLECTION AND ACTION

Reflect on and journal your responses to the following:

- What format would you like to use for your celebration bank?

- What do you already have that could go into it today?

- Where could you ask for additional feedback and testimonials today?

- What system or rule could you put in place to ensure that you regularly add to and build your celebration bank? An example of such a process would be to decide that once a month, every month, you will request at least one LinkedIn testimonial from a client, team member or colleague. Tie this activity to an already established monthly one so that you do not forget. Establishing a clearly defined process will help you hold yourself accountable.

- Where will you house your bank and how will you ensure that you remember to draw from it when you need to?

 **Key lessons**

In this chapter, you have explored reasons to keep sharing leadership and considered ways to ensure you remain on course as an inclusive leader. You have learned the following:

- Your saboteurs will keep showing up to try to derail your progress.

- That when you find yourself coming up with reasons why you cannot be inclusive, you must recognise and stop this blame habit and identify where you are possibly being defensive. Consider the learning you need to harvest in these times.

- The importance of prioritising the legacy you are building, not just for the future, but for today.

- The importance of preparing yourself to tackle periods when your confidence might get shaken and how your celebration bank can help in those times.

11
Future Focus

U p to this point, this book has been focused on preparing you to let go and share leadership so that you could build confidence in your people to step up and lead with you. Now we will move on to consider you and your team as one and learn how best to nurture and lead an engaged team of leaders.

Through the SHARE Leadership method, you have seen the importance of getting to know your people, harnessing their diversity, empowering them as individuals and collectively, and nurturing the leadership they have to offer. To fully inspire your people to embrace and sustain leadership, you must also ensure that they feel ownership of, and responsibility for, where your organisation is headed and understand their individual and collective roles in getting you there. With a strong sense of purpose, no longer looking to you to drive your collective journey, every individual will feel empowered to step into the driver seat as and when your organisation needs them to.

In this final chapter, we look at how you maintain shared leadership within your organisation. My hope is that you will then start to connect differently to the organisation that you and your people will co-create, feel less like you need to lead from the front and be inspired by the recognition that you are part of something bigger. As your people feel a powerful sense of co-responsibility for this renewed organisation, so will you.

Shared vision

One way to sustain shared leadership is to ensure that you and your people are aligned around your organisational vision. It is this vision that will drive forward your collective work, and shape your purpose, mission and strategy. The vision needs to be truly aspirational, stretching your organisation and all within it beyond their comfort zone. It will inspire enough to challenge and enthuse everyone to do and be better in service of your shared vision.

As an inclusive leader, your people need to share and understand your vision, build from it and have an active role in co-creating your mutual shared vision. Despite general awareness of this leadership requirement, all too often I find that professionals are unable to articulate their organisational vision, usually because it sits solely with their leader. To be truly inclusive, the vision needs to inspire and engage every individual in a way that motivates them to show up fully and give of their best every day.

There is a widely shared anecdote that brilliantly demonstrates the importance of building a strong connection between the individual's daily responsibilities and the organisation's ultimate aspirations. The story concerns President John F Kennedy in 1961 at his first visit to the NASA's headquarters. As he toured the site, the president came across a janitor mopping the floor. The president introduced himself and then asked why the janitor was working so late. The janitor's response is legendary: 'Mr President, I'm helping put a man on the moon.' As Jansen notes, 'The janitor got it. He understood the vision, and his part in it, and he had purpose.'[38] How inspiring!

In a one-to-one interview with a senior member of staff from a large global organisation, I asked where he saw himself in relation to where his organisation was headed. To my surprise, his resigned response was, 'I'd have to know where the organisation was heading to know that.' How would your people respond to that question? Would they be able confidently to articulate where their individual and team roles fit into your organisational vision?

When your organisational vision is clear and mutually agreed, everyone will feel like they are part of something bigger and they will focus their ambition beyond today. With a strong understanding of the importance of their individual part in 'putting a man on the moon', they will be inspired to show up in a different way in the work that they do. They will feel a greater sense of belonging and of ownership, and gain confidence that they are key to your organisation's future just as much as they are today. They will understand how their individual and collective contributions matter and ultimately, they will be more strongly motivated by the work that they do and be committed to giving their best.

Succession planning

Here is a fact that leaders often struggle to acknowledge: you are not going to be in your position and organisation forever. With that in mind, consider the extent to which you are preparing your organisation to continue your good work, to keep expanding and to stay competitive after you have gone.

When I worked in-house in financial services, I participated in and facilitated multiple succession planning meetings. I witnessed the anxiety that the process often triggered in senior leaders. Years later, not much has changed. At an external leadership conference with leaders from a wide range of organisations, I participated in a small group discussion, 'The Future of Leadership', where we talked about the newer generation of leaders. We discussed the growing speed of creativity and innovation and explored how organisations can make sure that 'old school' processes and systems do not inadvertently stifle progression. During the conversation, one leader courageously admitted that he found the process tough as it forced him to confront his fears about 'what's next for me when I'm pushed out by the ones coming up behind?' This anxiety came as no surprise to me as it frequently comes up in our executive coaching sessions, particularly when I challenge leaders to tackle their saboteur-driven insecurities which feed the urge to block the progression of their future leaders.

Organisations often do not do enough to develop leaders who empower others and work to build a legacy for themselves and a future for the company. Those organisations that recognise the need to focus on developing a sustainable and enduring leadership culture commit to a succession planning process which identifies, at an early stage, talented individuals who have the potential to step into key roles. Despite this, too often they do not do enough to equip their existing leaders with the confidence to let go and share leadership.

My experience of facilitating the succession planning meetings identified three issues that often stood in the way of effective succession planning:

1. Avoidance of the process by leaders. This reluctance often arose from fear because the focus on their talented, high-performing employees tended to trigger their saboteurs and induced feelings of Imposter Syndrome.

2. The process planned was not sufficiently inclusive. This can be avoided by asking questions that really force you to confront your diversity challenges and address this balance where it is needed. The following questions may offer a useful prompt:

   - Looking at the successors we have identified as 'ready in two years', how diverse is that list?

   - How reflective of our workforce and community is the succession plan?

   - If we are not yet sufficiently diverse and the list looks like a replication of our current leadership demographic, how can we address this? Who needs to review the list or be part of the selection process? What opportunities to develop those not sufficiently like ourselves have we missed? How do we rectify this imbalance?

3. A lack of follow-through on developing potential successors. This can be addressed by expanding the identification process to include a focus on development, considering each successor and asking questions like the following:

- For this future leader to be ready to step into their future role in twelve to eighteen months, what exactly will we do to prepare them and bridge the gap from where they are today to where we envision them being?

- What sacrifices and investments are we as leaders willing to make?

- How will we hold one another accountable to ensure that we have these future leaders sufficiently developed, empowered and included within the agreed timeframe?

 NUGGETS FOR REFLECTION AND ACTION

Reflect on and journal your responses to the following:

- Do you have a succession plan?
- When was it last reviewed by your leadership team?
- What development support have you provided to ensure your future leaders are ready for their next role within your predicted timeframe?
- Who might be threatened by their progression?
- What are you doing to minimise or even eliminate those feelings of threat and prepare those people to let go?

See your middle managers

All too often, the middle managers of an organisation are left underdeveloped and underutilised. This leaves the organisation in a vulnerable position as these middle managers have power even if they may not yet have full executive leadership. Fail to recognise this at your peril.

When culture change initiatives fail to stick, it is often due to a failure to engage the middle leaders. This is highlighted by research from *Harvard Business Review*, which notes that 'the positive impact of visionary leadership breaks down when middle managers aren't aligned with top management's strategic vision. This can cause strategic change efforts to slow down or even fail.'[39] The article counsels strongly against ignoring the potentially 'dark side' of the managers' visionary leadership but also outlines the clear benefits when this leadership can be appropriately engaged.

Kate Franklin is passionate about the potential of these middle managers and this led her to co-found Nkuzi Change, a company that specialises in providing focused development programmes 'to unlock the potential of Middle Leaders so that organisations and individuals can thrive'.[40] In a conversation between us, Kate explained that, having coached senior executives and teams for over twenty years, she had been struck by how ill-served the middle managers were in terms of dedicated and specialist training programmes. This has also been my experience of development offers across various organisations. Without the support of the middle managers, visionary leadership is too often thwarted and new initiatives fail. Nkuzi Change recognises that it is not enough just to prepare existing leaders to share. This must be complemented by focused and dedicated training of the future leaders to ensure that they are adequately prepared and supported to take the reins, embrace change and play an active role in transforming their organisations.

Take this a step further by considering how diverse your talent pool is. Look at progression data for your organisation and consider where additional sponsorship would be needed by those who have not had or do not have equal privilege of access to champions, role models they can identify with and opportunities. Learn to see, engage with and get to know your middle managers. They are powerful, not just as leaders in the future, but even in their current roles. Ensure you have alignment among your middle managers and engage them closely so they feel certain of, and ownership towards, your organisational strategy. Only then will you be able to harness and embrace all that they have to offer now, while simultaneously growing and developing this for the future.

 NUGGETS FOR REFLECTION AND ACTION:

Reflect on and journal your responses to the following:

- How do you ensure your middle managers are fully engaged and always aligned?
- How diverse is your pipeline and to what extent is your organisation harnessing and nurturing that diversity?
- Are there additional ways in which you could harness their full potential today?
- To what extent have you equipped your middle managers to step up?
- Do you provide dedicated and targeted support to develop their leadership potential?
- What more could you do?

 **Key lessons**

In this chapter, you have looked beyond your current leadership and organisation to consider what is needed to ensure your people stay committed to co-creating a diverse and inclusive future for your organisation. You have learned the following:

- The importance of co-creating your organisational vision and ensuring that everyone can understand how their role aligns with, and contributes to, that vision.

- Succession planning is a journey that requires you to not just identify potential, but to be prepared to let go and to develop your future leaders.

- Your middle managers play a crucial role in getting your organisation from where it is today to where it needs to be.

- Diversity at this middle management level is crucial and needs to be proactively encouraged and nurtured.

- As an inclusive leader committed to sustainable change, you will need to invest in your middle managers, ensuring they are given appropriate, tailored development and support to prepare them for their future leadership roles.

Conclusion

Let Go Leadership is hard. It is an invitation to look in the mirror, acknowledge those beautiful, comfy shoes that you always default to and step into bigger shoes that will always be hard to fill. Making that commitment to inclusion can leave you feeling vulnerable and insecure. It means accepting that you will have more questions than answers. You will keep developing by inviting difference, sharing power and becoming inclusive.

Being an inclusive leader is a journey, not a destination. The moment that you feel that your journey towards 100% inclusivity is complete is also the moment when you have stopped being inclusive. This is because being inclusive means committing to an ongoing movement through those five SHARE Leadership phases: regularly seeking feedback from all, having ongoing accountability, adapting your leadership to ensure that everyone is welcome, reconnecting with and engaging the diversity of your people, and empowering them to co-create with you from their own authentic selves. This is a cycle that the inclusive leader must undertake continually and can never consider complete.

Along the way, you will need reminders. To conclude, I would like to offer you the following guiding principles as you continue to let go, become more inclusive, share power and drive sustainable high performance in and through your people.

Ten guiding principles of Let Go Leadership

1. **Judge less, ask more.** Recognise that you are human and so imbued with inherent subconscious biases and affinities. Learn to recognise these and then set them aside. Make a conscious effort to reserve judgement on others. Where judgement occurs (your own and from others), interrogate it carefully to identify its true motivation. Come up with other perspectives you can explore the situation from. Try to build empathy by stepping into the shoes of others. Is your judgement something you wish to hold on to or could you now set it aside?

2. **Be careful about how and when you exert influence or convey your expectations, even unintentionally.** Try to retain a neutral position in your team interactions that require diverse thinking. This will allow true differentiation to emerge and allow you space to see your people, empower them more, and invite and welcome their contribution.

3. **Know when to use your skills and experience to teach, mentor or coach others**, and remember to ask questions to learn from others. Recognise that every team member carries a wealth of wisdom, perspective and lessons that you can learn. Ask more questions and invite feedback on your listening skills. It is not enough just to listen; you must also ensure that you are properly hearing what your people say and that you are understanding it correctly. Check regularly that your people feel heard and ensure that they recognise that their opinions and input are valued and taken onboard.

4. **Proactively build empathy.** Learn to see things from other perspectives and through the eyes of others. Imagine yourself as an employee within your organisation: what might you think and feel? Be open to letting these diverse experiences and opinions inform and influence you and your organisation.

5. **Say less and speak less often.** Learn to stay with silence: it is rich in potential and possibilities will

emerge if you provide a space that invites diverse thinking. Remember Nancy Klein's 'time to think' and consciously build in time to allow everyone equal opportunity to think and speak.

6. **Consider your privilege, get to know your people and learn more about intersectionality.** Think about ways in which you have more privilege than others; explore the times or ways in which you might have less. Be mindful of how you use your privilege and the power that it affords. Endeavour to use it to serve those who may have less and never abuse your power or let others abuse theirs.

7. **Create dedicated time and spaces for shared thinking.** Listen with a mind free of expectation or obligation. Make them spaces where all members feel equally valued and entitled. Be aware of the different ways in which people may respond in these situations, differentiating where required to offer tailored individual support and encouragement to ensure equity. Pay equal attention to what is not being said just as much as to what is. Notice those who are not speaking, or who do not feel empowered to do so: why is this and how can you address it?

8. **Be transparent with your people.** Commit to creating a culture of openness and regular communication, even when you may feel it is unnecessary. Do not forget the strength inherent in saying sorry, exposing your own vulnerabilities

and humanity, and drawing others in to support you. Share stories of who you and how you have come to be, creating connections and promoting authenticity in your people. Share what you can and be open when you cannot.

9. **Be fully accountable** – to yourself, to your people, to your decisions and to your organisations. Accountability cannot be achieved without inviting and accepting feedback. Both are powerful tools, not to be feared but to measure progress, impact and success, and to identify where your intentions do not translate to your impact. Practise identifying the voice of the saboteur and shutting down unhelpful thoughts when they occur, but also listening and learning from those around you, checking in with yourself frequently and holding yourself accountable to ensure that you have not slipped out of the SHARE Leadership cycle required for true inclusivity.

10. **Celebrate and reward inclusive practices.** Acknowledge and champion relationships, co-creation, collaboration and teach your team to blow your team trumpet.

As I reach the conclusion, my hope is that in reading this book, you have been inspired to embrace this journey to being an inclusive leader, understanding that it requires a lifelong commitment to ensuring inclusion in everything you do, within and outside of your workspaces.

I invite you to share the lessons you have learned from this book with others, whatever stage of their leadership journey they may be at. It is never too late to commit to making yours an inclusive leadership journey, and in doing so, you can inspire others along the way.

Ultimately, it is my dream that through this journey you will join us in a movement that, by means of many small ripples, is gradually creating a wave capable of generating lasting change and building a better, inclusive world, for today and for generations to come.

To stay connected with me and for more information and resources, visit my website www.obijames.com and sign up for our free blogs, videos and inclusive leadership assessments.

References

1 S Sandberg and N Scott, *Lean In: Women, work, and the will to lead* (Knopf, 2013)
2 R Lorenzo et al, 'How diverse leadership teams boost innovation' (BCG, 2018), www.bcg.com/en-us/publications/2018/how-diverse-leadership-teams-boost-innovation, accessed January 2022
3 'White Paper: Hacking diversity with inclusive decision making' (Cloverpop, no date), www.cloverpop.com/hubfs/Whitepapers/Cloverpop_Hacking_Diversity_Inclusive_Decision_Making_White_Paper.pdf, accessed January 2022
4 KO Conner, 'What is code-switching? Understanding the impact of code-switching for racial and ethnic minorities', *Psychology Today* (3 December 2020), www.psychologytoday.com/gb/blog/achieving-health-equity/202012/what-is-code-switching, accessed January 2022
5 V Hunt et al, *Delivering through Diversity* (McKinsey, 2018), www.mckinsey.com/business-functions/people-and-organizational-performance/our-insights/delivering-through-diversity, accessed January 2022

6   P Clarke, '"I'm in a dark place": Leaked Goldman Sachs survey shows just how stressful it is being a junior banker', *Financial News* (18 March 2021), www.fnlondon.com/articles/im-in-a-dark-place-leaked-goldman-survey-shows-just-how-stressful-it-is-being-a-junior-banker-20210318, accessed January 2022

7   'Groupthink', *Psychology Today* (no date), www.psychologytoday.com/gb/basics/groupthink, accessed January 2022

8   A Quito, 'A survey of 20,000 creatives suggests that brainstorming is a giant waste of time', *Yahoo! Finance* (15 January 2020), https://finance.yahoo.com/news/survey-20-000-creatives-suggests-132727299.html, accessed January 2022

9   WeTransfer, *Ideas Report* (WeTransfer, 2020), https://ideasreport.bywetransfer.com, accessed January 2022

10 JH Cho, '"Diversity is being invited to the party; inclusion is being asked to dance," Verna Myers tells Cleveland Bar', *Cleveland.com* (May 2016), www.cleveland.com/business/2016/05/diversity_is_being_invited_to.html, accessed 12 May 2022

11 *The Employee Burnout Crisis: Study reveals big workplace challenge in 2017* (Business Wire, 2017), www.businesswire.com/news/home/20170109005377/en/The-Employee-Burnout-Crisis-Study-Reveals-Big-Workplace-Challenge-in-2017, accessed July 2022

12 M Blanding, 'National health costs could decrease if managers reduce work stress', *Harvard Business School Working Knowledge* (2015), https://hbswk.hbs.edu/item/national-health-costs-could-decrease-if-managers-reduce-work-stress, accessed January 2022

13 C Maslach and MP Leiter, 'Understanding the burnout experience: Recent research and its implications for psychiatry', *World Psychiatry*, 15/2 (2016), 103–111, www.ncbi.nlm.nih.gov/pmc/articles/PMC4911781, accessed January 2022

14 KA Wade-Benzoni et al, 'It's only a matter of time: Death, legacies, and intergenerational decisions', *Psychological Science*, 23/7 (1 July 2012), 704–709, https://pubmed.ncbi.nlm.nih.gov/22692338, accessed January 2022

15 'Alfred Nobel', Wikipedia (last edited January 2022), https://en.wikipedia.org/wiki/Alfred_Nobel, accessed January 2022

16 'Alfred Nobel's Will' (The Nobel Peace Prize, no date),
    www.nobelpeaceprize.org/nobel-peace-prize/history/
    alfred-nobel-s-will, accessed January 2022
17 'Jamal Edwards: Tributes flood in for music entrepreneur',
    BBC News (2022), www.bbc.co.uk/news/uk-60457063,
    accessed 26 May 2022
18 ICF, 'Ethical standards in coaching', https://
    coachingfederation.org/ethics, accessed 19 May 2022
19 T Kellett, 'Attract and retain talent through reward',
    theHRDIRECTOR (15 July 2019), www.thehrdirector.com/
    features/reward-and-recognition/attract-retain-talent-
    reward, accessed January 2022
20 H Flippo, 'A well-known quote attributed to Goethe may
    not be actually be his', *ThoughtCo* (27 August 2020), www.
    thoughtco.com/goethe-quote-may-not-be-his-4070881,
    accessed January 2022
21 K Neff, 'Definition of self-compassion' (Self-compassion, no
    date) https://self-compassion.org/the-three-elements-of-
    self-compassion-2, accessed January 2022
22 SW Lazar et al, 'Meditation experience is associated
    with increased cortical thickness', *Neuroreport*, 16/17
    (2005), 1893–1897, www.ncbi.nlm.nih.gov/pmc/articles/
    PMC1361002, accessed January 2022
23 'Mindfulness-based stress reduction', Wikipedia (last edited
    January 2022), https://en.wikipedia.org/wiki/Mindfulness-
    based_stress_reduction, accessed January 2022
24 M Williams and Dr D Penman, *Mindfulness: A practical guide
    to finding peace in a frantic world* (Piatkus Books, May 2011)
25 S Gottfried, 'Niksen is the Dutch lifestyle concept of doing
    nothing – and you're about to see it everywhere', *Time* (12
    July 2019), https://time.com/5622094/what-is-niksen,
    accessed January 2022
26 J Zenger and J Folkman, 'The ideal praise-to-criticism ratio',
    Harvard Business Review (March 2013), https://hbr.org/2013/
    03/the-ideal-praise-to-criticism, accessed 12 May 2022
27 O James, 'Let's talk about race' (LinkedIn, 2020), www.
    linkedin.com/posts/obijamesuk_blacklivesmatter-activity-
    6674975307977564160-m0Ct?utm_source=linkedin_
    share&utm_medium=member_desktop_web
28 N Kline, *Time to Think: Listening to ignite the human mind*
    (Ward Lock, 1999)
29 'How we are creating the new language of leadership' (Co-
    Active Training Institute, no date given), https://coactive.com/
    about/new-language-of-leadership, accessed January 2022

30 L Page and S Brin, '2004 Founders' letter' (Alphabet
    Investor Relations, 2004), https://abc.xyz/investor/
    founders-letters/2004, accessed January 2022
31 S Kotler, 'Why a free afternoon each week can boost
    employees' sense of autonomy' (Fast Company, January
    2021), www.fastcompany.com/90595295/why-a-free-
    afternoon-each-week-can-boost-employees-sense-of-
    autonomy, accessed 12 May 2022
32 NI Eisenberger, 'The neural bases of social pain:
    Evidence for shared representations with physical pain',
    Psychosomatic Medicine, 74/2 (February 2002), 126–135,
    www.ncbi.nlm.nih.gov/pmc/articles/PMC3273616,
    accessed January 2022
33 Mind Tools Content Team, 'David Rock's SCARF model:
    Using neuroscience to work effectively with others' (Mind
    Tools, no date), www.mindtools.com/pages/article/
    SCARF.htm, accessed 19 May 2022
34 A Edmondson, 'Psychological Safety and Learning
    Behavior in Work Teams', *Administrative Science Quarterly*,
    44/2 (June, 1999), 350–383, https://journals.sagepub.com/
    doi/abs/10.2307/2666999, accessed January 2022
35 A Guha, 'Understanding triangulation: What to do when
    someone tries to draw you into a personal conflict',
    Psychology Today (4 October 2021), www.psychologytoday.
    com/us/blog/prisons-and-pathos/202110/understanding-
    triangulation, accessed January 2022
36 'Devil's advocate, n.', *OED Online* (Oxford University
    Press, December 2021), www.oed.com/view/
    Entry/54284170, accessed January 2022
37 'Equity, n.', *OED Online* (Oxford University Press,
    December 2021), www.oed.com/view/Entry/63838,
    accessed January 2022
38 T Jansen, 'JFK and the Janitor: Understanding the WHY
    that is behind what we do' (beqom, 26 November 2014),
    www.beqom.com/blog/jfk-and-the-janitor, accessed
    January 2022
39 NY Ates et al, 'Why visionary leadership fails', *Harvard
    Business Review* (28 February 2019), https://hbr.
    org/2019/02/why-visionary-leadership-fails, accessed
    January 2022
40 Nkuzi Change, www.nkuzichange.com, accessed January
    2022

Further Resources

Online resources

British Mindfulness Institute,
www.britishmindfulnessinstitute.co.uk

Co-Active Training Institute, https://coactive.com

CRR Global, https://crrglobal.com

CRR UK, www.crruk.com/what-is-orsc

The Gottman Institute, www.gottman.com

International Coaching Federation,
www.coachingfederation.org.uk

The NeuroLeadership Institute,
https://neuroleadership.com

Nzuki Change, www.nkuzichange.com

Self-Compassion, Dr Kristin Neff,
https://self-compassion.org

Team Coaching International,
https://teamcoachinginternational.com

Articles

Losada, M and Heaphy, E, 'The role of positivity and connectivity in the performance of business teams: A nonlinear dynamics model', *American Behavioral Scientist*, 47/6 (2004), 740–765, https://journals. sagepub.com/doi/abs/10.1177/0002764203260208

Books

Criado Perez, C, *Invisible Women: Exposing data bias in a world designed for men* (Abrams Press, 2019)

Downs, J, *Stand by Me: The forgotten history of gay liberation* (Basic Books, 2016)

Eddo-Lodge, R, *Why I'm No Longer Talking to White People About Race* (Bloomsbury, 2017)

Gottman, J, *The Science of Trust: Emotional attunement for couples* (WW Norton, 2011)

Gottman, J and Silver, S, *The Seven Principles for Making Marriage Work* (Three Rivers Press, 1999)

Olusoga, D, *Black and British: A forgotten history* (Pan Macmillan, 2016)

Patterson, K et al, *Crucial Conversations: Tools for talking when stakes are high* (McGraw-Hill, 2002)

Rosenberg, MB, *Nonviolent Communication: A Language of Life* (Puddle Dancer Press, 2nd edition, 2003)

Runde, CE and Flanagan, TA, *Developing Your Conflict Confidence: A hands-on guide for leaders, managers, facilitators, and teams* (Jossey-Bass, 2010)

Scott, S, *Fierce Conversations: Achieving success in work and in life, one conversation at a time* (Berkley Publishing Group, 2002)

Stone, D, Patton, B and Heen, S, *Difficult Conversations: How to discuss what matters most* (Viking, 1999)

Unerman, S, Jacob, K and Edwards, M, *Belonging: The key to transforming and maintaining diversity, inclusion and equality at work* (Bloomsbury, 2020)

Wilkerson, I, *Caste: The origins of our discontents* (Random House, 2020)

Acknowledgements

There are many people without whom this book would have remained a dream or turned out poorly. I will start with Dr Pirkko Ezewuzie, the best listener and coach I have ever known. I also happen to have connected with her even before I was born, because she is my mother. Thank you for always believing in me. Next is my dad, Dr Norbert Eze-wuzie, a great leader, role model and the one who inspired my love of business, authenticity and sense of agency. Rest in peace.

I want to thank my best friend, Ijey Spiropoulos, who is also a colleague, confidant, one of the beta readers for this book, and most importantly, my awesome sis-ter. Also my big bro, Patrick Ezewuzie, who always has my back and without whose reassuring presence in my life, I would not have taken many risks (including the writing of this book) that have propelled me forward.

Thank you to my other beta readers:

- Yvette Noel-Schure, you always know the right time to check in on me and always have the right words.

- Marianne Markowski, thank you for the invaluable time and attention to detail you put into checking the initial manuscript for this book and for bringing attention to structural inconsistencies that would have impacted its flow.

- Lisa Anderson, as a leader who had just transitioned into leading a new organisation at the time of reading the manuscript for this book, your feedback showed that you read the book with a commitment to share praise and challenge any unclear messaging, but also to apply its lesson. Your vote of confidence in this book was incredibly motivating and made all the difference.

- Stella Okuzu, your steadfast support, wise counsel and vision for this book came at a time when they were much needed. Your feedback on the manuscript hugely influenced my ability to pitch it at the right level.

- Sharmila Unadkat, thank you for sharing your successes, providing inspiration for this book and believing in its vision.

- Sonia Meggie, thank you for your friendship, belief and advocacy, for saying yes to being a beta reader for this book, and for championing my work.

Thank you to my other dear friends who have in unique ways supported, inspired and championed me over the years:

- Suniti Chauhan, boss-turned-friend and role model, for walking the talk of authentic leadership and teaching me so much.

- Nairy McMahon, who 'gets it' and continues to journey with me as we grow as inclusive leaders.

- Amelia Ventura, selfless friend and mentor whose support and guidance has inspired some of my best leadership decisions.

To all my colleagues and clients who have regularly provided opportunities for stretch and challenge, feeding my values of lifelong learning and, ultimately, for teaching me the lessons I share in this book. Thank you.

To Lucy, Joe, Vicky, Kathy, Hannah, Anke and the whole Rethink Press team, you are the best midwives a book could ever have! Thank you.

Finally, I would like to thank my greatest friends – 'Dope Women' – Anne-Rose Obidi, Tina Ogundipe, Kome Brown and Mmaezi Nwogu, for being my haven during the most trying time of my life, and before, during and beyond the writing of this book.

Finally, to Yosra El-Essawy, thank you for your legacy. I miss you.

The Author

Obi James is a Finnish-Nigerian Leadership Expert committed to creating inclusive cultures of shared leadership and empowered relationships, in which every individual can thrive.

With extensive experience of successfully developing leaders and teams across large multinational organisations, including Morgan Stanley, Deloitte, Bank of America and Northern Trust, she left corporate employment in 2012 to set up Obi James Consultancy and has since successfully trained, mentored and coached leaders, partnerships, teams and organisations globally through periods of uncertainty, change and cultural transformation. Her clients have ranged from public to private sector businesses, including Barclays, Bloomberg, BlackRock, Visa, Lloyds, Co-Op, Sony Music, FARFETCH, Save the Children and the NHS.

Obi dedicates much time to coaching executives and senior leadership teams. She is a sought-after facilitator and speaker on women in leadership, antiracism, allyship and inclusion at international corporate events such as the Global Finance Transformation Summit, Women in Banking & Finance (WIBF) Strategy Day, and Bloomberg's Multicultural and Senior Women's Forums.

In 2019, she was elected to become a council member and trustee for Royal African Society, where she works to facilitate its mission of amplifying African voices and interests globally. She is a judge for the annual Business Book Awards and the StartUp Awards National Series. Obi has won global industry awards for her work on leadership and for her dedication to inclusion.

🌐 www.obijames.com

f www.facebook.com/obijamesuk

🄳 @obijamesuk

🄾 @obijamesuk

▶ www.youtube.com/c/ObiJames

Lightning Source UK Ltd.
Milton Keynes UK
UKHW020445231022
410948UK00017B/163